# FAMILIAR FACES, HIDDEN LIVES

HOWARD BROWN, M.D.

# Familiar Faces
# Hidden Lives

## THE STORY OF
## HOMOSEXUAL MEN
## IN AMERICA
## TODAY

Harcourt Brace Jovanovich

New York and London

Printed in the United States of America

Library of Congress Cataloging in Publication Data

Brown, Howard, 1924–1975.
Familiar faces, hidden lives.

Includes bibliographical references.
1. Homosexuality—United States—Personal narra-
tives.  2. Homosexuality—United States—Case
studies.  3. Gay liberation movement—United States.
4. Brown, Howard, 1924–1975.  I. Title.
HQ76.3.U5B7      301.41'57'0973      76–24910
ISBN  0–15–130149–2

First edition

BCDE

# CONTENTS

# FAMILIAR FACES, HIDDEN LIVES

# CHAPTER ONE

# A Public Figure

As the day neared on which I was to be sworn in as the chief health officer of New York City, I found myself faced with a problem: What should I do about Thomas? We had been living together for five years. The swearing-in ceremony at City Hall on the morning of June 3, 1966, would be the crowning point of my career in public medicine. As the city's first health services administrator—a post created by Mayor John Lindsay, which I had been chosen to fill by a panel of public health experts—I would be in charge of coordinating the programs of the Departments of Health and Hospitals, the Community Mental Health Board, and the office of the Chief Medical Examiner, and I would also serve as Commissioner of Health. I wanted, naturally, to share the day's joys with Thomas. I wanted him to be at my side as I was driven to City Hall in my limousine—one of the perquisites of office which, with its siren, telephone, and special insignia, every new commissioner takes a kind of childish pride in. I wished that he could sit in the place of honor traditionally given at such ceremonies to members of the new commissioner's family and that he could stand beside me in the receiving line at the party afterward. I knew he could not. The question was: Could we afford to be seen together at all?

I obviously passed as a heterosexual in the eyes of the Mayor and the panel; otherwise they would not have selected me. On the other hand, shortly after my appointment was announced, at least one newspaper described me as "a forty-two-year-old bachelor who lives in Greenwich Village"—which I took to be a readily translatable journalist's code for "gay." Such allusions frightened me. Of course, I had lived for a long time with the fear of being "discovered." Every homosexual has lived with this fear and—at least until the advent of gay activism—has timidly learned to accept it as the way things are. In my situation, however, as I was about to take up a position that would almost certainly involve me in a great deal of controversy and publicity, the slightest allusion to my homosexuality shook me. Becoming more visible in my profession meant that I would have to try even harder to conceal this important part of my life.

I took what I thought were adequate precautions. Thomas and I did ride down to City Hall together in the chauffeured limousine, but when we arrived he slipped out one door and mingled with the crowd while I stepped out the other, to where my sister, whom I had asked to stand in for the wife I didn't have, and her two children were waiting for me. It was Jule and her children who sat among the guests of honor and stood with Mayor Lindsay and me in the receiving line after the swearing-in ceremony. When Thomas walked by, I smiled and shook his hand as if he were just another well-wisher.

If I had had time to really think about it, I probably would have refused the job. The risk of being exposed while in office was simply too great, and my exposure could

4

well discredit or impair health care programs whose success mattered more to me than my own career. But events outran discretion. Less than six hours after I had been suggested for the job, Mayor Lindsay was asking me if I could manage it, and impetuously I said yes.

For some weeks I had been providing the chairman of the Mayor's search committee with information about the three city departments—those in charge of administering the city's hospitals, mental health services, and public health programs—that Mayor Lindsay proposed to integrate. The other, more prominent officials who could have supplied this information were all candidates for the new post; I was not. But one afternoon in mid-May, as we were leaving a conference at Rockefeller University, the chairman asked me if I would be interested in the job myself. Taken by surprise, I said yes. Half an hour later we were at City Hall meeting with the mayor's counsel, Donald Elliot. Did I think I could put together the three city departments? I said that yes, I did. "Well," he said, "you're the first person I've spoken to about this job who thinks he can."

Heading up this new three-in-one department was not going to be easy. I knew that. Two very experienced health leaders had already turned down the job on the grounds that the agencies involved would fight being integrated, thereby making the new administrator's life a daily hell. But the possibilities for improving health care programs, especially for the city's poor, were great. This had long been my main interest; indeed, it was my small-scale achievements in this field that had brought me what little fame I enjoyed. In 1962, as director of the Gouverneur Ambulatory Care Unit on Manhattan's Lower East Side, I had established a model neighborhood health center program that had attracted the attention of health officials throughout the country. In 1964, largely as a result of my work in this poverty-stricken neighborhood, I was appointed chief medical adviser to the Office of Economic Opportunity in Washington, D.C. While continuing as director of the Gouverneur unit, I helped set up similar neighborhood health care centers in Watts, California, Mount Bayou, Mississippi, and some half-dozen other cities. Also during the early '60's, I had taken part in a campaign to compel New York City to build a new Gouverneur Hospital. (The clinic had been built around 1917, the hospital in the 1890's.)

The facility I had in mind was, again, an innovation—a community-centered hospital in which family doctoring would be stressed—one, in short, that would integrate the public health and mental health facilities with the actual curative services of hospitals. Once the city had agreed to support this project, I set out to see what each of the various health care agencies was doing in my neighborhood and to see if I could consolidate their efforts. My study took three years. In the process, I accompanied public health nurses on their home visits, made the rounds of most of the city's health facilities, and talked with health department and hospital officials on all levels.

It was my knowledge of the workings of the various city health care agencies that had made me useful to the Mayor's search committee and that now accounted for my conviction that these agencies could work together, as I had been so quick to tell Donald Elliot.

At six o'clock that evening I was introduced to Mayor Lindsay on the steps of City Hall. Then Elliot, the Mayor, the chairman of the search committee, and I climbed into the Mayor's limousine and set off for Gracie Mansion, his official residence. By the end of that half-hour ride, Mayor Lindsay had designated me his new health services administrator.

John Lindsay and I had never met before, but we had

instant rapport. For one thing, we shared a number of concerns. We were both indignant about the kind of care poor people were receiving and about the way they were being treated by health professionals. Lindsay, too, had toured the city hospitals, visited neighborhood health facilities for the poor, and listened to complaints about the shortage of doctors, the long waits on hard benches in bleak waiting rooms, the gruff impersonality of many staff members. Lindsay was a reformer who wanted change—and fast.

And there was reason to believe that change was possible. The previous year, as part of President Johnson's Great Society program, more health legislation had been passed than ever before. Medicare would provide money for the aged, Medicaid for the poor; special grants would be available for new programs for working mothers and their children and for new neighborhood health centers. Yet I got the impression that the Mayor had found the city's medical establishment less than enthusiastic about making prompt use of these new means. He seemed to have found it hard to talk with establishment doctors. I was an outsider with whom he could speak freely. In a sense, we saw ourselves as allies about to take on the establishment.

"How's your health?" Lindsay asked toward the end of the ride.

"Fine," I said.

"Well, do you think you can handle the doctors?"

"Yes."

"Then you're the man I want."

And so, apparently, a few hours of talk, culminating in this brief conversation with the Mayor, had radically changed my life. At noon I had been the director of a small hospital in one of the city's worst ghettos. Soon I would be overseeing the administration of twenty-two municipal hospitals, twenty-three district health centers, ninety-four child health stations, and many other programs. I would be overseeing 50,000 city employees and an annual budget of nearly one billion dollars.

I say "apparently" because after we had all left the Mayor and gone off to the Plaza Hotel for drinks—I needed one—and dinner, none of us could quite believe what had happened. Even after the first round, we were still so astounded that Don Elliot went to a pay phone and called the Mayor to ask: "Are you sure you've offered the job to this guy?"

Within a few days, the Mayor's search committee had endorsed me; ten days after that, I was sworn in, and a private man, who had so far succeeded in keeping his homosexuality a secret, became a public figure.

I later heard from homosexual friends in the city administration that rumors about me began to circulate on the very first day of my new job. Some people had seen me arrive at City Hall with another man. Others had noticed Thomas and me together that afternoon at a reception at the United Nations (my sister had had to take her children home). Since Thomas was a physician, though not involved in public health, and had none of the attributes of the stereotypical homosexual, I had naïvely thought that no one would find our being together strange.

If I behaved recklessly that first day, I was on the whole fairly cautious. I could see that it would be risky now for Thomas and me to go on living together. He moved into an apartment around the corner. There was rarely time for us to have dinner together; I often got home from work too late to be with him at either his apartment or mine. And the dinner parties I was now invited to all the time, I was invited to alone. There was no time to visit any of my gay friends.

On the other hand, I knew many homosexual physicians,

and it was a great relief to be able to see them in the round of meetings, hospital tours, and social events that made up my official day. Through them I met a number of other homosexuals in high positions in the Lindsay administration.

Like most homosexuals who work together, we were bound by our common need to hide. We could not be too careful. We could not talk in our official cars because of the chauffeurs. We came to be wary of telephones— a secretary might pick up while we were talking, or our phones might even be tapped. One gay commissioner regularly sent a technician around to check out my office telephones. The technician also taught me how to set the screw on the wallbox so that I could tell if my phones were bugged. At home, I had two telephones, one of which was connected to an answering service My commissioner friend warned me never to use the service phone to call a homosexual and never to speak of homosexuality—the operator might be listening in, and if anyone did want to tap me, it was the service phone he would probably choose. My other phone was, like my office phones, regularly checked out by the commissioner's assistant. The anxiety involved in taking such precautions practically canceled out the reassurance that the all-clears were supposed to provide.

The group of homosexual city officials I came to know never dared to meet socially as a group. If word of a gathering of unmarried men from various city departments had got around, people would have wondered what common interest had brought them together. And, of course, our only common interest was that we were gay. On rare occasions a few of us got together at one another's houses with our lovers. In our official lives, which often extended long into the night, we had to maintain a front. Some of us were able to pass as heterosexual by producing girl

9

friends or wives as credentials; others, like me, were forced to appear more or less neuter. At our small, relaxed, and all-too-infrequent parties, we could drop the pose and talk about our real lives, our real friends, and about such otherwise taboo topics as cooking. As we entered and left one another's houses, we worried about being seen and taken for couples. We seldom dined out.

One summer night, though, three of us—all in the field of public health—decided to dine with our lovers at a Greenwich Village restaurant. The two other officials' lovers were much younger than they and were not connected in any way with either the Lindsay administration or public health. Shortly after we had been seated, I looked up and saw a party of women prominent in public health walking toward our table. I rose, stammered out introductions, and sat down, wretched that we had risked dining out at all.

A fair number of the homosexuals I knew in the Lindsay administration held high positions. There were some homosexuals in both Mayor Lindsay's small cabinet of deputy mayors, administrators, and budget directors and his large cabinet, which included all city commissioners and assistants to the Mayor. Several of these homosexual officials made important and innovative contributions; many others were pedestrian; and at least one was generally considered a weak appointment. I should add that I myself did not appoint any homosexuals to important jobs, not because there were no qualified candidates, but simply because I lacked the courage.

Lindsay and I worked well together. Then, suddenly, in December, six months into my new job, there was a crisis. One day as I was going into the Mayor's office, Don Elliot took me aside and said he had to speak to me about something "very important" as soon as possible. I didn't have time that afternoon, and I was giving a speech in the Bronx that evening. He asked if he could come to my apartment that night. He arrived at about midnight, walked into my living room, sat down, and, after a moment of embarrassed silence, said: "There's a rumor that you're having a homosexual love affair with———," naming a member of the Mayor's administration. "I don't know why it should matter," Don went on, "but is it true?"

I, too, had heard this rumor. I could honestly deny it. Then Don asked, "Is there anything about you that is going to embarrass the Mayor?" Again, I honestly denied that there was. I had never been arrested, and unless some detective broke into my apartment or my lover's while we were actually making love, I was convinced I never would be. Don and I went on to discuss some city business. As he got up to leave, he said: "I suggest you forget tonight and act as if it never happened."

I couldn't forget, of course. His questions had terrified me. And not just the questions but also the specter that had raised them. Had the Mayor himself heard rumors about me and sent Don as his envoy? Although I could not accept Don's advice to "forget tonight," I had no choice but to carry on as if nothing had happened. I was not in a position to raise a fuss, to search out my anonymous accusers and clear my name. I realized that the real issue here was not whether I happened to have had a homosexual affair with a member of the Mayor's administration, but whether in fact I was homosexual.

Shortly after this midnight visit, a gay commissioner told me that he had just come from the Mayor, who had called him in about a rumor that the commissioner was accepting payoffs. The commissioner had effectively refuted the charges. Yet even after Lindsay's assurance of confidence in him, my friend had worried aloud that his reputation would be damaged. Finally, the Mayor said, "Don't worry. Some people will say anything. A few weeks ago they were saying that Howard Brown was a homosexual."

Evidently, then, Mayor Lindsay did not believe the rumors about me. The subject never came up again during my time in office, and the Mayor remained as cordial to me as he had been before his counsel visited me. If he had believed the story Don Elliot questioned me about, I do not know what he would have done. Mayor Lindsay was not particularly sympathetic to homosexuals, although many New Yorkers assumed the contrary, since during his administration the police did not harass homosexuals. Under previous mayors, handsome young policemen had gone out on the streets to entice homosexuals and arrest them when they responded. Lindsay considered this a violation of the civil rights of homosexuals, as well as a debasement of the policemen involved. (I will never forget being taken, in my capacity as night Mayor, on a tour of the Tombs, Manhattan's grim house of detention, by the Commissioner of Corrections, and shown the section reserved for homosexual offenders. Almost all the men in the crowded cells were demonstratively effeminate. I could not identify with them, and I froze, too terrified to ask any questions about their treatment.) During the Lindsay administration, police raids on gay bars were all but abandoned, on the grounds that it was better to allow homosexuals to congregate in bars than to have them roaming the streets. And in 1972, Lindsay issued an executive order prohibiting discrimination based on "sexual orientation" in all municipal appointments. But his support for legislation introduced the same year that would have barred such discrimination city-wide—in employment, housing, and public accommodations—was nominal. He neither spoke out for the bill nor used his influence to get it passed. As a result, it did not even get out of committee. (In 1974, when at last the City Council voted on it, it was defeated 22 to 19, with two abstentions.)

One reason for the Mayor's rather slack stand on this issue was, I believe, a simple lack of understanding. He could not see homosexuals as ordinary people faced with the daily need to conceal their sexual identity. In general, his concept of sexual matters was simplistic. In his world, men naturally played the dominant role in sexual relationships, as they did in society. He once took it upon himself to explain to me why a certain woman we knew, prominent in city affairs, was so restlessly active. Her constant bustling and concern meant that she was sexually on edge. He knew the woman's husband and was sure that he could satisfy her in bed, so why didn't she calm down? Again, when he heard that one of his sharper critics, who happened to be a single woman, had rented part of her apartment to a bachelor, he said that maybe now she would stop sniping. His comment, of course, implied not only that her criticism had been based merely on frustration, but also that any woman who allowed a man to live in her home inevitably wanted him to bed her.

The disparity in the ways we looked at sex did not impair our working relationship. I, playing the part of the professional neuter, smiled and laughed in all the right places, and got back to the task at hand. Enjoying the Mayor's full support, I was able to accomplish quite a bit —at least in the first few months of office. We drew up plans for the construction of some thirty neighborhood health centers for poor communities; we began a crash program to cheer up and clean up the city's hospitals. We recruited new architects—the old ones wouldn't go along with my plans—to design what I called one-class-care hospitals that would do away with wards for the poor and have instead only private or double rooms—hospitals with freshly painted walls and air conditioning, designed to meet the needs of all income groups. (My basic building policy remains in force. All city hospitals, starting with those begun in my time, will have either all private rooms or mixed private and double rooms.)

This initial flurry of activity soon subsided into a period

of waiting—waiting for paper plans to become projects. I soon found myself bogged down in a number of drawn-out conflicts. I wanted to set up quality-of-care standards for Medicaid patients. Practicing physicians categorically opposed such standards; medical schools, on the other hand, wanted to see them even higher. The New York State Department of Health, which had the final say, struck out some of my requirements and, after I had left office, struck out even more. What was left was a gutless set of standards acceptable to the medical establishment. Another hassle developed when Congress made comprehensive health planning mandatory. The established voluntary Health and Hospital Review Council of Southern New York wanted to administer this program. Mayor Lindsay and I agreed that a new public planning agency should be set up to give due representation to minorities and the poor. Predictably, the council, a bulwark of the traditional white power structure, opposed our plan, attacking it in public meetings and debates and, privately, in homes and hospital corridors all over town. (A "straight" city official later told me that many of my opponents used my rumored homosexuality as a way to discredit me, since this was easier than finding fault with my stand. It was not until after I left office that the issue was resolved and a public comprehensive health planning agency was established.

These were, admittedly, conflicts that any administrator would have to learn to live with. But I was new to the job—especially to wielding so much power—and the job itself was new. (Its ability to devour its occupants is attested to by the fact that the two highly professional public health men who succeeded me were both fired after holding office for about a year and a half each.)

Added to these pressures were the fears engendered by the recurrent rumors of my homosexuality and the strain my duties continued to place on my relationship with Thomas. In December 1967, I came down with infectious hepatitis, a disease of the liver that leaves one weary, weak, and depressed, as well as jaundiced. At first, thinking I was only coming down with a cold, I continued to go to work. It took me some time to diagnose my own illness, and when I did I checked right into St. Vincent's Hospital. The next day my brother-in-law, John Sibley, a reporter for the New York *Times*, visited me in the hospital and told me a story that made me decide to resign. Apart from my sister, John was the only heterosexual who knew that I was homosexual. He told me that he had just come from a *Times* city-section editorial meeting at which the new investigation Drew Pearson was working on had been discussed. The year before, Pearson had written a series of articles about homosexuals in the administration of California Governor Ronald Reagan, and it now looked as if he were going to expose homosexuals in Mayor Lindsay's. My brother-in-law went on to say that in the course of the meeting, reporters had accurately listed every homosexual prominent in the Lindsay administration. John recited the names to me; I listened, stunned. Our supposedly private lives were, if not yet public knowledge, no longer secret.

The next day I sent Mayor Lindsay my letter of resignation.

This was, I realize now, the act of a man exhausted, sick, and close to despair at the thought of seeing his career ruined and his high hopes of doing some good for society shattered. It is one thing for a reporter to know that a man is homosexual, and quite another for him to use that knowledge to bring down a public official. Pearson could never have proved anything against me. No incriminating pictures existed; I had never been arrested for committing a homosexual act. But my thoughts did not run along these logical lines. I saw myself accused of being myself, and I felt utterly defenseless.

Lindsay visited me at St. Vincent's. We talked for nearly an hour. He refused to accept my resignation. I suggested other public health leaders who I felt would be stronger and more effective than I. He wanted none of them. He reminded me of our common desire to give the poor the same kind of care as the rich. I assured him that I felt as strongly about this as ever, but that I simply could not go on. It never occurred to me that I could tell him my real reason for stepping down. He left bewildered by my resignation.

In time I came to see that that visit was full of ironies. I knew John Lindsay to be a compassionate man with a real concern for the rights of minority groups. My own concern for minority rights was deep and long-standing. In the '40's, when I was attending medical school, I had campaigned and plotted for weeks to get a Jewish student pledged to a fraternity that had traditionally barred Jews. (My ruse was to get the dean of the medical school to congratulate the fraternity for its wise decision before the fraternity had voted. It worked: after that, they couldn't back out.) In the early '50's I had served as one of the first full-time doctors at the United Auto Workers' clinic in Detroit. I came from a conservative, basically antiunion family, but my experience with UAW officials —an impressive bunch of men—and my discovery of the exorbitant fees most practitioners charged my working-class patients were enough to radicalize me on health care issues. And I had come to know and admire many black civil rights workers in the later '50's and throughout the '60's, when I helped to fight the injustices the poor had long suffered at the hands of a callous medical establishment and a society uninformed and indifferent. And yet in 1968, although I was well aware that I belonged to a minority myself, it did not occur to me that I had rights or that my confinement to a life of secrecy and fear was a wrong to be protested. Or that I could speak openly with this mayor and friend whose civil rights stand I admired.

As it turned out, Drew Pearson never published his Lindsay administration exposé, so I need not have resigned. But the mere threat of exposure had been terribly demoralizing. Perhaps, I thought, I had to topple and break before I could put the pieces together again and—replacing dread with courage this time—publicly announce my homosexuality. This was to take five years and a close brush with death.

The announcement, which I made on October 3, 1973, in an address to some 600 physicians at a symposium on human sexuality held at the Carrier Clinic in Belle Mead, New Jersey, ended my life of fear. More importantly, through subsequent television interviews and massive newspaper and magazine coverage, it helped to open up a public dialogue on homosexuality focusing on the problems and rights of homosexuals. It brought me thousands of letters from homosexual physicians, homosexual medical students, homosexual lawyers, homosexual teachers, homosexual clergymen, homosexual farmers, homosexual mechanics, homosexual policemen—homosexual men from every level of society. The very variety of my correspondents lent proof to my conviction that society's picture of homosexuals was absurdly distorted and needed to be corrected promptly; only this could dispel society's destructive attitude toward a large segment of the American population and secure for them their civil rights, including the freedom to love fearlessly.

The Kinsey Report—published in 1948 and still the best study of American sexual behavior—estimated that 4 per cent of white American males were exclusively homosexual. The report adds, however, that "25 per cent of the male population has more than incidental homosexual experience or reactions ... for at least three years between the ages of 16 and 55," and that "37 per cent of the total male population has at least some overt homosexual experience to the point of orgasm between adolescence and old age."*

Homosexuality, then, is likely to be a matter of some concern to every American family. Although I always prided myself on being primarily a family doctor, first for poor neighborhoods and then for one of the largest cities in the world, I could never bring myself to speak up on this important matter. Now that I have come out, I feel I must.

* Alfred C. Kinsey, Wardell B. Pomeroy, Clyde E. Martin, *Sexual Behavior in the Human Male* (Philadelphia: W. B. Saunders Co., 1949), pp. 623, 650.

CHAPTER TWO

# A Public Stand

If I had publicly announced my homosexuality in 1968, when I resigned from the Lindsay administration, I would have found little understanding and even less support. I would probably have had to commit suicide the next day. By 1973, such a thought was wildly out of date: Both the attitude of homosexuals toward themselves and the public's attitude toward them had changed. And one of the events that triggered this change of atmosphere had occurred only a four-minute walk from my Greenwich Village apartment.

At 3:00 A.M. on June 28, 1969, the police raided the Stonewall Inn, a gay bar at 53 Christopher Street. They had a search warrant authorizing them to investigate reports that liquor was being sold at the unlicensed private club. Homosexuals had long had the reputation of being easy to push around—as had blacks and American Indians before they began to fight for their civil rights, as had Jews before the Israeli army took on the Arabs. And the group of some 200 homosexuals that the police proceeded to expel from the Stonewall Inn was by and large effeminate.

But then an unexpected thing happened. Regrouping at nearby Sheridan Square, they started to taunt the police, then to throw anything they could lay hands on at them —bricks, bottles, garbage, even a parking meter. The riot lasted for forty-five minutes. Thirteen rioters were arrested and four policemen injured. It was the first time homosexuals had united to fight back against men whom they had come to see as their oppressors. They were not fighting for any clearly defined rights. Caught up in a seemingly irrational fury, they had simply exploded.

For the next two or three nights, Stonewall homosexuals gathered to taunt the police on Christopher Street. My front windows were open, and I could hear the shouting. Curious and anxious, I walked over to watch the demonstrators. They were like the homosexuals I had seen in the Tombs—most of them obviously poor, most of them the sort of limp-wristed, shabby, or gaudy gays that send a shiver of dread down the spines of homosexuals who hope to pass as straight. I could not have felt more remote from them. And yet, at the same time, the scene brought to mind every civil rights struggle I had ever witnessed or participated in.

The riots broke a spell. Gay activism grew out of Stonewall. Young homosexual radicals, many of whom had worked with Students for a Democratic Society throughout the country, together with a group of jobless, rootless New York City gays, went on to form the Gay Activists Alliance in December 1969. Taking over from where the Stonewall rioters left off, they began demonstrating and otherwise pushing hard for changes in the law that would secure for homosexuals their right to live and work without discrimination.

In the fall of 1970, New York University offered me a dual appointment at the Graduate School of Public Administration and the School of Medicine. (After resigning as health services administrator, I had spent two years as visiting associate professor of community medicine at the Albert Einstein College of Medicine in the Bronx and as director of community medicine at two Bronx hospitals, where I hoped to create new health care programs. These were not productive years. The nationwide swing back to a conservative health policy made things difficult for me. Also, I was depressed by having had to step down from public office.)

New York University is in Greenwich Village, which had naturally become the center of gay activism. Shortly after I started to meet my classes, undergraduate homosexuals demanded that the university allow them to hold gay dances on campus. I took it for granted that the administration would reject this demand. But talking with other professors, I was astonished to find almost unanimous support for it; the only question was whether the undergraduates should be allowed to invite nonuniversity men! The predominantly "straight" faculty was more ready to support gay rights than I was—a fact driven home to me by a brief, cordial grilling from a colleague.

"What do you think?" he asked me. "Should the gays get their own dances?"

"No," I said. "I'm not in favor of them."

"Well, why not? Do you think homosexuality is contagious? I mean, you're a doctor. Do you really think it'll spread all over campus if they get to dance together?"

"No, of course not."

"Then, why not let them dance?"

To bring the conversation quickly to an end, I said I saw his point. But the episode stuck with me. My reaction had revealed that I was so ashamed of my sexual identity and so bent on preserving my heterosexual pose that I could not even think logically. Fortunately, the issue did not need my support: The gays were allowed to hold their own dances on campus, and nonstudents were allowed to attend.

21

Although I still felt unprepared to associate myself openly with the gay activist movement, I did want to help in some way. By assisting bolder people, I hoped to atone for my behavior. Thus, later that fall, when a young activist lover of a physician friend of mine asked if I would raise money for the Gay Activists Alliance, I said I would. I knew many rich homosexuals. It was the least I could do.

Most of the men I approached contributed—but only after insisting on certain conditions. Afraid of writing out a check to an organization with the word "gay" in its title, they would write out checks only to me. And I had to agree to make sure that their names would not be put on any mailing list. What I now saw as their excessive timidity —just a few weeks before, I would have been equally circumspect—inspired me to take my first small step toward freedom: I wrote out a check to the GAA and signed my name with a flourish. To hell with the bank.

Though willing to contribute, none of my rich homosexual friends and acquaintances were willing to join me in actively working for gay liberation. And I badly needed company. The world of the young activists was totally different from mine. Poor, often living communally, bright but with little formal education, they looked to me for money or medical assistance; they could not give me the moral support I needed as I stepped haltingly from total concealment. We didn't speak the same language, we didn't know the same people. They rejected the respectability I had worked so hard to achieve.

At that time I still accepted many of the psychiatric clichés about homosexuals—that we were emotionally impaired narcissists who could never love as fully as heterosexuals, that we were innately superficial and irresponsible. And as I stood alone, between two seemingly opposite groups of homosexuals, my sense of the inherent inferiority of homosexuals was reinforced by the behavior of both groups. Didn't the fact that many of the young activists couldn't or wouldn't hold down jobs and lived on welfare prove that they were irresponsible? And didn't the inability of my older, established friends to see the crucial civil rights issues involved in the gay liberation cause show them up as shallow?

These doubts served a strategic purpose: They allowed me to postpone taking a stand. I continued to solicit contributions and to contribute to the gay movement myself, and I continued to vacillate.

In June 1972, I had a heart attack and was taken to St. Vincent's Hospital once again. In spite of heavy sedation, I could not sleep that first night. I was forty-eight years old. Almost everyone in my family had lived to seventy-two. I hoped to live at least that long. I knew, as a physician, that if I survived the first week, my chances of recovery would be good. It was during that sleepless night that I first accepted the reality of death and found that I was not afraid to die. And I saw that if I could overcome this greatest of all fears, I should also be able to overcome the fear of standing up to declare and defend my identity as a homosexual. And since my life, I realized now as never before, was finite, I had better act soon. Also, I knew that if there was one legacy I wanted to leave, it was to have helped in some way to free future generations of homosexuals from the agony of secrecy and the constant need to hide. Here, again, the work would have to begin soon.

The next day the sedation took effect, and I slept for a full forty-eight hours. I woke feeling refreshed; presently my room filled with visitors—young activist and middle-aged friends. My doubts about both groups dissipated. My old friends appeared to me now as my real family, and in the activists I saw the beauty of the courage that sustained them in their struggle. I would leave the clichés to the psychiatrists. My visitors left me with no doubt that we homosexuals were entitled to the same right to be open and proud of our identity as all other human beings.

It took me all summer to recover from my heart attack. From the fall of '72 on, I edged my way toward coming out publicly. Looking back, I can see that a large part of the process was finding role models—homosexual men engaged in the movement with whom I could talk as an equal, men who could provide me with an example. This was not easy. One thought that ran through my mind was, incredibly: If I come out, what will my secretary say? This was a worry no one in the activist movement could begin to share; none of them had secretaries. I was helped out of these quandaries by three men I met—men who, in responsible positions themselves, could sympathize with my petty concerns as well as with my larger ones.

The first was Henry Messer, a neurosurgeon associated with the Mattachine Society, a center for the dissemination of information about homosexuality set up in 1955 and generally regarded by young activists as an Uncle Tom organization. Dr. Messer not only participated in marches and demonstrations but also was involved in giving a course on homosexuality for rookie policemen at a Greenwich Village precinct. By the spring of 1973, after attending a couple of these classes, I felt free enough to tell his students that I was a homosexual. And on June 28, I marched with him in the Christopher Street Liberation Day parade commemorating the Stonewall riots of 1969. Slowly and unsurely, I was coming out.

A second key figure was Martin Duberman, the forty-three-year-old Distinguished Professor of History at Lehman College, City University of New York, and the author of *In White America*, an off-Broadway success of 1963 and 1964. While recuperating from my heart attack I had read Duberman's book *Black Mountain*, which describes the great years and the decline of an experimental educational community in North Carolina, a refuge for such artists and thinkers as Buckminster Fuller, Paul Goodman, Robert Rauschenberg, Merce Cunningham, John Cage, and Charles Olson. Duberman's mentioning his own homosexuality in the book was his way of coming out publicly. I was particularly affected by his rendering of the lonely departure of Black Mountain's rector, Robert Wunsch, in 1945, after he had been indicted for "crimes against nature," or homosexual acts, and released on suspended sentence.

After release from jail, Wunsch waited, as agreed with the Board of Fellows, until one o'clock in the morning before coming back to pick up his things; and, as was also agreed, he then slipped away for good before the community awoke.... To this day Molly [Gregory, a senior officer in the college] regrets that as she lay awake that night and heard "those little feet go back and forth, back and forth, carrying books," she resisted the impulse to go downstairs and offer Wunsch her help—"because I'd been told I shouldn't."*

No one helped the former rector pack or move out. No one even said good-bye to him. He drove off in a roadster, Duberman writes, and has not been seen or heard from since. The truth had not set this educator free; it had finished him.

Whenever I thought of keeping silent about myself for my own sake, this story inspired me to come out for the sake of all homosexuals. So, too, did Duberman inspire me. I discovered he was a neighbor, and we became close friends.

The third figure who helped me step forward was Bruce Voeller. He is tall, lean, and boyishly handsome, an accomplished skier, swimmer, and horseman. In 1961, while working for his doctorate at Rockefeller University, he

* Martin Duberman, *Black Mountain: An Exploration in Community* (New York: E. P. Dutton, 1972), p. 231.

married; he and his wife proceeded to have three children. It was only after his divorce a few years later that Voeller, at the age of thirty-eight, had his first homosexual experience. He is now on leave from the university to serve full time as president of the Gay Activists Alliance.

The main reason it had taken him so long to realize his sexual identity, Voeller explained, was that he could not identify with the stereotypical image of the homosexual man ("homosexuals had to be effeminate"). Then, too, it was convenient not to believe that he was homosexual. But, as Voeller emphasized, a man's failure to discover his sexual nature before he married could result only in bitterness and pain for both partners. Voeller concluded that the misleading and destructive stereotype would have to go, and to get rid of it, more homosexuals in all walks of life would have to come out.

By the time I met Voeller I was already looking for an occasion to come out that would be politically effective. I did not want just to state a fact; I wanted my message to make a dent in public opinion. Then in July, Dr. Messer called to say that he had been invited to address a gathering of physicians at a symposium on human sexuality in New Jersey and suggested that perhaps I, too, should address them. The occasion seemed exactly right.

Three weeks before I was to deliver my address, I told the board of directors of the New York City Public Health Association, which was considering appointing me chairman of a committee to combat discrimination against homosexuals in the health community, that I was homosexual. They appointed me chairman. Here again, as at New York University, I was surprised by the tolerance among heterosexuals.

When the symposium was only a few days away, the GAA press secretary sent out a release stating where and when it was to be. I doubted that the media would pay any attention: I was now a professor, not an important city administrator—and, anyway, press releases from homosexual organizations are generally overlooked.

The symposium opened with a series of films of people engaged in every kind of sexual behavior—heterosexual intercourse, oral-genital heterosexual sex, homosexual sex, masturbation, bestiality, sadomasochism, and so on. The purpose of this was to desensitize the participants so that they would feel free to talk openly about sex. Suddenly a message was flashed on the wall saying that there was a telephone call for me. Doctors are accustomed to being summoned on emergencies, but I had not been in practice for years. I emerged from the dark auditorium to find myself facing ranks of television cameras. All the major networks and wire services were there. I answered their flurry of questions—"Why did you announce your homosexuality?" "Will you name other prominent homosexuals?" "Do you think homosexuality is an illness?" "What about homosexuals molesting children?" "Have you ever been discriminated against?"—and returned to the theater in time to watch a heterosexual couple engage in cunnilingus.

I was glad the media had taken note of my stand. On the other hand, I still had to face all the physicians in the huge auditorium. As I watched the explicit sex in film after film, I wondered how my speech would be received. A film on female masturbation left me feeling like a middle-aged prude. Next to me sat the person I had driven out to New Jersey with that morning, who was also giving a speech that afternoon. We both planned to talk seriously to the assembled group of doctors about the right of homosexuals to be treated as ordinary human beings. We were worried that our earnest speeches might be a letdown after the "action" of the films.

I was very tense at the beginning. The organizer of the symposium, Dr. Richard Cross, chairman of the department of community medicine at Rutgers Medical School, had suggested that first I establish myself as "just another doctor"—a physician talking impersonally about homosexuality—then jar them with the news that "I was invited here not as a medical scientist but as a homosexual. I am publicly announcing my homosexuality in the hope that it will help to end discrimination against homosexuals."

The glaring lights of the television cameras set up in front of me prevented me from seeing my audience. With the cameras whirring, I could not tell how my audience was taking my statement of a fact I had felt forced to keep secret for more than thirty years.

Dr. Cross had told me that he wanted a homosexual doctor to speak on homosexuality so that "physicians would stop thinking of homosexuals as just hairdressers, interior decorators, and male nurses." This was a point I, too, wanted to drive home. "I have met far more homosexual physicians than I have homosexual nurses," I began, "more homosexual politicians than homosexual hairdressers, more homosexual lawyers than homosexual interior decorators. One of my best friends, for example, is a former All-American football player, a Stanford graduate, and now the president of a large New York advertising firm. I have homosexual friends who would be regarded as humanitarians, just as I have homosexual friends who have narrow and limited interests. Members of the gay activist groups have been beaten up by the police and sent to jail for their activities, just as civil rights activists were in the sixties. But I also know homosexual policemen who have been among those arresting gay demonstrators."

I pointed out that the studies establishing homosexuality as a disease or pathological abnormality were not convincing, and went on to explain why—as I shall do later in this book. I concluded by urging my audience to do its part to free this generation of homosexuals from the fears and agony so many of my generation suffered.

28

The doctors applauded. But I was still tense, wondering how the newspapers would treat the story and how my friends and the public would react.

Back in New York, I was interviewed briefly for an evening newscast. The science reporters, some of whom had roundly criticized me as health services administrator, now congratulated me on having had the courage to come out. I returned home to find that my telephone recording service had picked up scores of encouraging messages from friends and colleagues as well as requests from television interviewers to appear on their shows. As for the press, the New York *Times* treated my announcement as front-page news. This surprised me, since the *Times* had generally avoided mentioning homosexuality except in its science columns, where it was invariably referred to and discussed as an illness. It appeared that people could like me even when they knew I was homosexual, and that I had made my dent after all.

Yet the full impact was still to be felt—in the letters that literally began to pour in from all over the country— letters of support, letters from people in hiding, letters from parents or wives of homosexual men.

Here are extracts from a few of them.

From a New York City housewife:

Five years ago my husband realized he was homosexual. He has been tormented ever since, although my understanding and acceptance have helped him to some degree. We are separated now and, strangely, closer than ever in many ways. He visits our children as often as he wishes; the door is always open for him. Although I know that we will never again live together as man and wife, I also know that we will always love each other.

My heart breaks for him and for others in his predicament.

I want people to open their eyes and realize that homosexuals are human, too. I want to help free homosexuals from the mental tortures society inflicts upon them.

From a teacher in Virginia:

The newspaper quotes you as saying that your decision to come forward was based, in part, on what you see as a sharp drop in public hostility toward homosexuals. I imagine that that is true in New York City and probably along the New York–New Haven–Boston axis. But in the rest of the country—apart from San Francisco and a few spots here and there—the old hostility is still very much alive. In Virginia at least, this is certainly the case. The Richmond papers do not hesitate to denounce "queers" and "fags" on the editorial page. This must seem incredible to anyone who takes the free air of New York City for granted.

I can only say that for a professional in a Virginia college—or for a teacher in any of the tax-supported schools in the state, for that matter—a disclosure like yours would result in instant dismissal. I would probably end up working in a dime store or a florist's shop.

From a man in Chicago:

I am a forty-seven-year-old executive so terrified of being found out and so guilt-ridden that I have avoided all sexual contact for the past fifteen years. Until I read of your announcement, I saw my life coming to a dead end, with nothing but total loneliness in store for me as the protective barriers of my immediate family fall away. I see now how foolish this has been, and I feel sufficiently heartened to attempt to develop a warm relationship with one person—a relationship that could sustain us both through the years to come.

You have shown me that being a "queer" does not mean that my life must be a succession of gay bars, washrooms, and bathhouses. If only more of us had the courage to speak out, we could accept ourselves and one another as human beings.

From a man in California:

We have been second-class citizens too long. My life has twice been traumatically interrupted. After serving as a naval officer for eight years, I was discharged during the McCarthy era as a security risk. At that time anyone could turn your name in as a gay and you were thrown out. There was no trial: you didn't even have to be caught "in the act." Twenty-two years later, after having worked ten and a half years with a computer firm, I was terminated because my supervisor, who hates homosexuals, found out I was gay from seeing my dishonorable discharge. I want to prevent such things from happening to younger generations of homosexuals.

It is to these people, and to the many others who are involved with them or merely curious about them, that this book is addressed. In it, I will describe my own experiences—how it felt to discover I was homosexual, how I found friends and lovers, how law, psychiatry, and religion affected my life and how they affect the lives of other homosexuals, including lawyers, psychiatrists, ministers, priests, and rabbis. And I will write of the lives ordinary homosexuals lead, and of the problems they continue to face, in America today.

If we all were to stand up in your midst, would you "always have known"? I doubt it. Sexually distinct we may be, but most of us are surprisingly like you.

# CHAPTER THREE

# Discovery

I was eighteen when I first perceived myself to be homosexual. I was taking a shower in my college dormitory. I looked at a naked boy and was sexually excited. The sight of other boys had excited me sexually before, but this was the first time that I connected my response with the word "homosexual." A straight-A student, I was, in this respect, a slow learner.

Being sexually excited by the sight of another boy made me aware that I was different, that "there was something wrong with me." I had never met a homosexual man, or at least been aware that I had met one. But I knew what every other Midwesterner knew in 1942: Homos were mysterious, evil people, to be avoided at all costs. And I was one. Often, when I thought of this, I would break out in a cold sweat. I couldn't be. I shoved the idea aside. When it cropped up, I thought: I must be the only homosexual in northern Ohio. It took me five years to discover that I wasn't.

Small Midwestern towns—close-knit, tight-lipped, and conservative as a Mason jar—are wonderful places to grow up in, up to a point. I grew up in a number of them. My father was a civil engineer who changed jobs frequently. By the time I went off to college we must have lived in half a dozen small towns in Ohio—places like Newark, Cadiz, Ravenna. Everyone in them was married and had a family, except for the occasional bachelor who had been jilted in his youth and the occasional old maid who had never been asked. Boys grew up to be men— he-men. And the first manly tests a boy had to pass were out on the diamond or the football field.

I flunked these tests. I threw a baseball like a girl. I struck out. I fumbled the high pop fly that any four-year-old could have caught while unwrapping a Mars bar. In football, while I could tackle and block, I couldn't pass well or catch well or kick at all. I tried my hardest; I sweated profusely and felt weak—the same symptoms I experienced when I had my heart attack. I was numb with terror, a terror based on a barely conscious awareness that social acceptance depended on athletic prowess. To flub was to be excluded from society, or at the very least ridiculed.

Because I was a dud on the playing fields, I strove to prove I was a man in every other possible way. I mowed lawns, delivered papers, built a tree house, put up a hoop and practiced basketball. And during my high school years I dated girls regularly, albeit out of a sense of duty. It was boys who interested me. I remember being so attracted to one boy—we were both twelve—that I followed him on my bike, always keeping far enough behind so he didn't notice me.

My father, not surprisingly, called me a sissy. He did not like having a sissy for a son. We had been very close when I was young; he used to take me along on his construction jobs. Then he began to complain that I didn't want to go out and play "like a real boy," and the rift

33

opened. A cousin of mine who *could* play baseball and football became his surrogate son. My father was as friendly toward him as he was now cold toward me. He stopped taking me along on his jobs, then stopped talking to me altogether. He did not attend my graduation from high school, my graduation from college, my graduation from medical school, or my swearing-in as health services administrator. This silent, hostile man became a specter that haunted me for years.

The hostile or withdrawn father was properly balanced, in my case, by the dominating or seductive mother—the close-binding mother, to use Dr. Irving Bieber's term. She was a poet of sorts and wrote articles that occasionally got published; she loved good books and she was religious. But it would be too simple to say that I was bound just to my mother. It was the whole world that women in my family stood for that gained my respect. My mother and my three aunts were all writers, scholars, teachers. They were kind, sensitive, and generous. My father was frequently hostile to my mother as well as to me, occasionally vicious to the point of sadism. (Toward my younger sister, he was tender and loving. Having failed to produce "a real boy," he was relieved to find that Jule was "a real girl.") Neither he nor any of my uncles cared about books or religion. They spoke contemptuously of "kikes" and "coons" and "fairies" and had no sympathy for the poor ("The poor have poor ways," they said). My mother spoke of the need to love everyone, and during the Depression she fed the many beggars who came to the door. Undoubtedly, it was she who sparked my concern for improving the health care of the poor.

I set off for college, a very naïve young man in a sexually simple-minded era—the beginning of the forties—in proverbially the most strait-laced region of America. How naïve was I? Well, some months after my revelation in the shower room, a student threw his arms around me and

34

said he loved me, and it never occurred to me he might be homosexual. I was vaguely aware that homosexuals were supposed to be effeminate, and he wasn't. Our friendship remained platonic.

I had entered Hiram College on a prelaw scholarship, but in my last year there I decided to become a doctor. I reasoned that I could not become a lawyer because I found it hard to talk to people, a difficulty I attributed to the fact that I had a secret: "Something is wrong with me." What exactly was wrong I did not know. I was sexually excited by members of my own sex, yes, but on the other hand I remained unconvinced that I was a queer because I did not find myself sufficiently disgusting.

I applied to Western Reserve Medical School in Cleveland in 1943 and was accepted, but before I could matriculate I was drafted (then discharged a year later to resume my studies). Shortly before I entered the army, in a moment of panic, I took a train up to Cleveland to discuss my sexual dilemma with the aging chairman of the department of psychiatry at the medical school. He told me I couldn't possibly be homosexual. I was going to become a doctor, wasn't I? Homosexuals didn't become doctors; they became hairdressers, interior decorators, that sort of thing. He explained away my urges as "delayed adolescence." The following year, his mission of enlightenment completed, he retired.

Coincidentally, this quack diagnosis was reinforced when a friend pointed out to me on a Cleveland street the first "homosexuals" I had ever seen. They wore makeup and their hair was waved. Whatever else I may have been, I was not one of those.

But in my third year at medical school I discovered that although I might not have looked like a fairy or felt as disgusted with myself as I should have, I was a man who enjoyed making love with another man.

Frank was tall, good-looking, relaxed, self-confident. He,

too, came from a small town. But where I was close only to my mother, Frank was close to both his parents. We belonged to the same fraternity. I lived in the fraternity house; he lived off campus. Presently I took to going over to his room to study. It was quieter there. And for several months we both really did study.

Then, by chance, we found we were reading the same novel—Gore Vidal's *The City and the Pillar*, a book about homosexuals. The characters in it were the first homosexuals I could identify with. Indeed, this novel was the first written evidence I had come across that there were other homosexuals like me. Very tentatively Frank and I discussed the book in relation to ourselves. We both confessed that there were times when we suspected we might be homosexual—but then we would vacillate and say it was impossible. He suggested that if we studied very hard and never again mentioned the subject, it might just go away. We tried that. We even walked or jogged for miles —I had been on the track team at Hiram—to wear ourselves out. But "it" did not go away. Rather, my fondness for Frank grew. At times he would say, putting his arm around my shoulders, "We're just buddies. We can't be queer."

One evening while we were studying in his room, Frank put his hand on my thigh. At first I thought that he was testing me. But his hand moved higher up my thigh. Then he threw his arms around me and said, "You're going to be my lover." I embraced him and we made love.

That was in 1946. I was twenty-two. I had found a lover —and one, furthermore, whom I respected and admired.

And now we met in his room not to study but to make love. We knew enough to conceal our relationship from the other students. When we met at the fraternity house we tried not to appear overly friendly. We took care to have dates for fraternity dances. We stopped taking our afternoon runs and long evening walks together.

Neither of us knew how to arrange our life as a homosexual couple. The situation was novel for us, and we had no guide. My feelings ranged from wanting a sort of formal engagement to wondering whether we should seek therapy. I wanted to bind Frank to me forever because, in those pre-Kinsey Report days, I could hardly believe that there were others like him. At the same time, I did not have to worry about his being faithful to me; neither of us knew any other homosexuals. When I suggested we both see a psychiatrist, Frank was puzzled—didn't we love each other and didn't we get along in bed? He took our affair in stride. It was I who worried about the future: We would be ruined if our secret were discovered; we might even have to commit suicide, like one of the characters in Vidal's novel.

My anxieties and confusion led me into a bit of *Catch-22* thinking. To coax Frank into seeing a psychiatrist, I would start by establishing that I was emotionally disturbed, then lead him to admit that anyone who could love a man as disturbed as I was must be disturbed, too. I began by saying that with parents like mine, I couldn't be normal. But Frank only laughed; in a teasing way he allowed that I probably was crazy, but said he loved me anyway. I then pointed out that all the books in the library that mentioned homosexuality treated it as a perversion, a form of neurosis. Frank replied that he didn't consider himself neurotic in the least. He had had a very happy childhood and he got along well with his parents, and if that didn't fit in with what the textbooks said, too bad for them. He was not going to start feeling guilty just because books told him he ought to. And so he eluded me at every turn. Finally, though, I developed an explanation for his refusal to visit a psychiatrist: Healthy and happy as Frank might *appear* to be, he was simply too disturbed to realize how disturbed he was.

I did not tell Frank of this lunatic conclusion. He would

only have laughed, and I did not regard this as a laughing matter. Indeed, our relationship broke up over the issue of psychotherapy. I marched off to the new chairman of the department of psychiatry and told him that I was homosexual. This one didn't mention hairdressers. He counseled me to quit medical school at once and go into analysis. And I would have, if I could have afforded it. As things stood, I was too poor. I was already working part time to put myself through school, since my father had refused to pay for my education and the school would not give me a scholarship because his income was sufficient. A full-time salary—even without tuition to pay— would never have been enough to support me and a psychiatrist as well. So I finished medical school, though later I spent four years in analysis.

Frank's casual acceptance of his nature took him a different route. During his interneship in another city, he met a stockbroker and they formed a long-term relationship. The stockbroker decided to become a doctor, too. By this time I was on the faculty of a medical school, and I was able to help Frank's lover get accepted. The two now share a practice in Denver.

Years after I left medical school, I discovered that Frank and I had by no means been the only homosexuals on campus in our day. In various cities, I encountered and talked with several. Many of them had felt even more isolated than we. Only one or two had been lucky enough to find a partner in their class. Most had since formed long-term relationships with other homosexuals. The few who had married continued to have sporadic affairs with men.

At medical school we had, supposedly, enjoyed advantages denied most homosexuals in those days. Homosexuality was at least spoken of in one class—although only fleetingly and in rather primitive terms. (The new head of our department of psychiatry was a Freudian, with the result that homosexuality was now described as a stage in sexual development that preceded heterosexuality.) There were counselors, men with doctorates in psychology and psychiatry, only a short walk from our guilt-ridden rooms. And we had access to a modern medical library, whose medieval definitions and findings I will be exhuming in my chapter on psychiatry. These, then, were the advantages we enjoyed, and in the midst of them we were woefully uninformed and unutterably lonely. Hiding from heterosexuals, we simultaneously succeeded in concealing who we were from one another. And, of course, the homosexual physicians on the faculty hid, too. Thus, there was not a single older homosexual we could talk to or in whose life we could find a model on which to pattern our own. We were a doubly lost generation.

Homosexual men discover their sexual nature in a variety of ways and at a wide range of ages. Some have been happily married for years when they find, abruptly or gradually, that their sexual relations with women leave them unsatisfied and that it is men they crave. Others engage in homosexual acts for years before realizing—or admitting to themselves—that they are homosexual. (This is not as strange as it may sound. The Kinsey Report points out that many men who go on to lead completely heterosexual lives have had some homosexual experience in adolescence. The report found that among male college students, about 45 per cent had at one time or another engaged in homosexual acts. Thus, such behavior does not, in itself, indicate that one is or will become homosexual.) In both cases, the realization generally comes as a shock. And an overwhelming feeling of loneliness is invariably part of that shock.

Victor is the forty-seven-year-old head of a progressive school and the author of two well-received books on educating youngsters. The eldest son of a Midwestern Protestant minister, he considers his Victorian childhood to have been generally happy. His mother was overly affectionate. His father, although somewhat remote, was neither hostile nor insensitive, and was as indifferent to sports as he was interested in music and literature. Victor had his first homosexual experience when he was sixteen and a prize-winning pianist participating in a summer music seminar at the state university. Even after having a prolonged sexual relationship with another young man, though, Victor did not consider himself homosexual. Realization came in college when he fell in love and had a months-long affair with a man. But love did not bring only relief and joy. Raised to regard homosexuals as monsters, he could not help loathing himself. For five years he considered suicide. He often read the Bible to find if God's love were large enough to include such sinners as he. He found no unequivocal answer.

To add to his feelings of guilt and confusion, girls kept falling in love with him: He was not only charming, intelligent, and gifted, he was also handsome. He could not bring himself to explain to any of them why nothing sexual ever happened between them. He could only hint that he was keeping a mistress in another city. (Many homosexuals face this problem. Posing no threat to women, and almost overly considerate of them, perhaps partly because they realize that they must eventually cause pain, they attract women who have grown weary of aggressive men.)

One summer when Victor was home for a vacation, his mother found a stack of letters from his lover in the East. At the end of a grueling interrogation by both parents and a prayer meeting with them, Victor promised to consult the church's psychiatric adviser in the East Coast city where he lived. The psychiatrist turned out to be homo-

40

sexual himself and more interested in Victor than he ought to have been. Victor fled from psychiatry. He was nearly forty before he accepted his homosexuality. Now his widowed mother—who fervently prayed while her minister husband read up on psychology—lives in the East with Victor and his present lover. Since she does not see what she does not want to see, Victor says, the arrangement works very well.

To judge by the letters I have received and by friends' reports, Victor's years-long contemplation of suicide is typical of many homosexuals who discovered their sexual identity in the forties and fifties. I know that during my college years, whenever I heard that someone had committed suicide, my first thought was: I wonder if he was homosexual.

Compounding the fearful loneliness that accompanies discovery is the general absence of role models. Blacks, of course, felt this same lack until the advent of their civil rights movement. People become, in large part, what they perceive they can become—a perception that depends on their knowledge of what others like them have become. And homosexuals have been a people almost totally without a history. Moreover, the fragments of history that do exist are still largely kept from the view of the general public. High school teachers generally do not mention Leonardo da Vinci's sexual proclivities, or Walt Whitman's or Oscar Wilde's or Henry James's or E. M. Forster's or W. H. Auden's; they usually treat the homosexuality of ancient Greece as classified information, if they are familiar with it at all. This concerted hush is hardly surprising, of course, since the administrators who run most high schools shy away from sex even in its traditionally most acceptable form. (In part they are yielding to pressure from parents, who yelp whenever the topic comes up outside the home—where it almost never does.)

The adolescent who learns nothing about homosexuals

in his formal education—informally, of course, he learns quickly enough that "queer" or "fag" or "homo" or "fairy" is the ultimate insult—picks up a picture of them from television. Effeminate speech or behavior always brings a roar of canned laughter, which is presumably echoed in the living room or "family area." (A good loud laugh at a queer is always proof of one's masculinity—and the more one doubts, the louder one laughs.) The TV faggot, of course, is as demoralizing to the adolescent homosexual as the movies' all-eyeballs-and-teeth-and-no-brain (but with a natural sense of rhythm) step-'n'-fetchit was to the adolescent black: Am I fit only to be laughed at? The noble queer, the queer who has made a contribution to society—the very idea may bring a smile to the reader's lips. The word "queer" does the trick—it's even funnier than "nigger."

When it comes to characterizing homosexuals, novelists and playwrights, usually an iconoclastic lot, stick pretty close to society's stereotype—think, for instance, of the homosexuals depicted in *Tea and Sympathy*, *Death in Venice*, and *Catcher in the Rye*.

Where then, can the young homosexual turn for a model of what he might become? So-called educators hold out a piece of paper on the back of which has been scrawled the American graffiti "homo" or "fag." So-called entertainers hold out a caricature and say, "Laugh!" Authors create a portrait of an aging loner or a weakling or a moral freak. The law threatens with a mug shot: "If we catch you making love with a person of your own sex, you'll wind up like this." Clergymen—too often twenty years behind the psychiatrists, who themselves have yet to catch up with the facts—solemnly extend the right hand of fellowship while suggesting that the afflicted lad seek professional guidance. If, in his need, the young homosexual should cry out for help to some older homosexual in town, he would probably find that nobody would dare to look up from his work and answer the call. And deafest of all would be the homosexual teacher, the homosexual cop, the homosexual clergyman, the homosexual doctor, or the homosexual psychiatrist. To come openly to the young man's rescue would mean having to pack up that night. Men who might not only provide counsel and reassurance but also serve as models for living see themselves as an endangered species. Chameleon-like, they have survived by assuming the coloring of their straight surroundings. And so they don't lift a finger.

This brings us to another stage in the painful process of discovery: Many homosexuals cannot believe that they are homosexual because they cannot identify with the stereotype. I could not identify with the drag queens I saw on that Cleveland street; Bruce Voeller, an accomplished athlete, could not identify with the effete men he recognized as homosexual. The stereotype—whose purpose, I suppose, is to reassure sexually anxious American he-men —prevented us from realizing that we were he-men in the literal sense of the word.

Another classic aspect of discovery is that it often comes after years of homosexual experience. The act of sex and the act of recognition—"So that's what I am!"—are not always synchronized. They were not in my case, or in Bruce Voeller's. Or in the cases of scores of the homosexual men who wrote me. Larry's life provides a dramatic example of this time-gap phenomenon.

Larry is a hearty, stocky, thirty-eight-year-old greengrocer who loves to eat and whose main topic of conversation is food. The only son of a woman who was widowed when he was three, Larry grew up in the Bronx. He had his first sexual experience at five, with a neighborhood boy a year older. In his teens, he had sex—generally mutual masturbation, but occasionally oral-genital contact as well

43

—with other willing boys in the neighborhood. ("A lot of kids my age didn't have any sex life at all," Larry told me, adding that his was a predominantly Catholic neighborhood, which meant that "girls were hard to get. They were all supposed to stay virgins until they got married.") Larry did not consider himself homosexual because so many other boys did the same things he did. "Anyway," he said, "queers were supposed to dress up in dresses and wear makeup and that kind of thing, and we weren't like that. Hell, we laughed at queers."

When he entered high school, Larry started to date girls while continuing to have sexual relations with boys. At nineteen, he was sleeping regularly with a girl. He liked her and he "liked having sex with her—but there was something missing." A year later, in Manhattan, he visited a gay dance bar for the first time.

Shocked by the sight of men dancing together, Larry stayed long enough to be impressed by the fact that most of them, who were roughly his age, looked as if they came from backgrounds similar to his own. As he put it, "It was sort of like the same crowd I'd known in the Bronx when I was a kid, but grown up." There were other differences. These young men did not consider themselves straight. Also, they did not just want to have sex; they expected to give and receive affection. Some had formed long-term relationships with other men. One of them, who had just broken up with his partner, asked Larry if he was living with anyone. The idea had never entered Larry's mind. Live with a man? A man lived with a woman.

Larry's former sexual partners from the neighborhood had all gone straight; many were married by now. He returned again and again to the gay bars of Manhattan, where he could always be sure of finding someone for a part of the night. Some of the homosexual men he met in the bars accustomed him to the novel thought that sex could include tenderness and affection. He became close friends with a young man, also from a lower-middle-class background, who had no doubts about his sexual identity.

One night, taking the subway back to the Bronx, Larry suddenly realized that "if that kid was a homosexual, so was I. But that was terrible. I mean, that meant I was a fairy, a queer, and some of my pals back in the Bronx once beat up a fag, a guy with bleached hair and a fruity walk. That was me?" He simply could not figure out how he fit into the picture. Or what the picture really was. As a boy, he had learned to spot and sneer at one set of characteristics —the effeminate set. But few of the men he met at the gay bars were effeminate. And they were all young. Did you get effeminate as you got older? Then, too, where were the older homosexuals? Had most of them committed suicide?

Baffled in many respects, Larry was at least and at last sure of one thing: He enjoyed having sex with men much more than he ever had with women. He subsequently moved into an apartment with a young man, with whom he lived for ten years. I asked Larry when he had finally decided that he was homosexual. He replied, "I'm not certain I ever have."

Recently, although perhaps only in isolated instances in a few areas of the country, young homosexuals have found it somewhat easier to accept their sexual identity. Information on homosexuality is certainly much easier to come by now than when I was young. Gay activist groups, service groups, and social groups exist in many large cities and on many college campuses, offering counsel and companionship—another significant change since my ill-advised, lonely years of discovery and doubt and denial. Furthermore, all across the country, a handful of men who crack the stereotype are lending a new sense of dignity and direction to young homosexuals.

Alex is a young man who, in some ways, is representative of the new breed of homosexual men. It is his complete cool that is representative, not his background, for he is certainly an exceptional young man—a boy who went on to be elected president of the student body of his Ivy League college, an honors graduate who was promptly offered an important job with the United Nations. Well, if he is unusual, so is his story.

Alex called me from his office a few days after the story of my coming out appeared in the *Times* and said he was curious to know just what had made me do it. The following day he dropped by my apartment to continue the conversation. We talked more about his life than about mine, however. His was more interesting. With Alex's permission, I turned on the tape recorder, as I had the night Larry came by for dinner.

Alex said that his first inkling that he was homosexual came from seeing a two-part series on homosexuality in *Life* when he was in the eighth grade. The articles did not strike him as being related to his own life in any way, but they stuck in his mind. Some weeks before this, his father had sat him down and told him about sex and reproduction: "a very liberal discussion, and all framed in the reference of love. 'When two people love each other, they . . .'—that sort of thing." This discussion made Alex feel free enough to mention that he had read the *Life* articles and to ask his father about homosexuality. As Alex tells it, his father said: "Oh. Do you remember what I explained to you about love and, uh, reproduction a few weeks ago? Well, basically, homosexuality is when two men feel the same kind of thing about each other, except that their relationship is unnatural."

Later, alone, Alex thought: "Maybe I'm a homosexual" —which wasn't an unusual reaction for him to have, he explained, because every time he heard or read about a sickness, he imagined he had it. "For instance, earlier that year I had seen a TV program on leprosy; I had athlete's foot at the time, and I convinced myself that the cracked skin between my toes was the first stage of leprosy. If I read about something, I started to feel all the symptoms."

In the ninth grade, Alex wrote a term paper on Mary Renault's *The Last of the Wine*, in which he devoted two pages to a discussion of homosexuality, "since two male characters in the book seemed to have the kind of relationship I'd read about in *Life*." His attempt to find research materials brought him up against himself for the first time. "I went to a couple of public libraries and I'd look up homosexuality in the card catalogue, and I'd find that you had to ask the librarian for the books, and I just couldn't do it."

Alex had a steady girl friend in his junior and senior years of high school. "I never had sex with her. I never wanted to. I didn't really think about it. Perhaps I kept myself busy doing other things so I wouldn't have to think about it."

Alex's freshman year at college was uneventful. As a sophomore, however, he made many new friends. Meanwhile, his highly developed social conscience impelled him to start a rehabilitation program in a nearby state prison which included encounter groups for the inmates. One prisoner participant came to Alex for help with "a problem that was tearing him apart. He told me that he had begun to sleep with another guy in prison, and he was afraid he was going to be queer when he got out." Alex, who was still a virgin, could speak only from his inexperience. His advice was, as he recalls it: "I can't see anything especially bad or unhealthy about it. And if you like the person, and having sex with him makes you feel good, relax. When you get out of prison, try sleeping with a girl. In prison you just don't have much choice."

That year Alex wrote a term paper on homosexuality in prisons that lent weight to his offhand advice. He found, among other things, that the majority of men who have homosexual relations in prison do so from need or, sometimes, under duress, and that they pick up their lives as heterosexuals when they are released.

A few months later, Alex was elected president of the student body; also, he fell in love with a classmate. In February, they set off for Stowe to visit a girl they both liked. On the way, they spent a night in a motel. "We were in the same room and I couldn't sleep and Rufus couldn't sleep. And I said, 'You know, Rufus, I've got something to tell you.' And he said, 'Yeah?' and got up and came over to my bed. I said, 'I think I'm in love with you.' 'Yeah?' he said. And that night we slept together for the first time."

I asked Alex if, later perhaps, he had worried about being homosexual. "It never made much sense to me to worry about it," he answered. "My only concern was, I loved somebody. It could probably have all turned out differently, but it didn't. I mean, I just never had time to fall in love with anybody until I went to college, and when I finally did, it was all the more intense—and it happened to be with somebody of my own sex. And love was the only thing that mattered."

# CHAPTER FOUR

# Coming Out

Back in 1947, when my relationship with Frank broke up, "coming out" meant letting a few other homosexuals know that you were one, too. You had come out of the closet and into, if not the world, at least the shadowy subworld of the gay bars. Nowadays, "coming out" means giving up any effort to conceal your homosexuality.

I came out in the old sense in the fall of '47. I had worked hard during the summer, getting my obligatory months of obstetrics out of the way—learning how to deliver babies by delivering them. I lived in at the maternity wing of the Cleveland University Hospital, where I was on call twenty-four hours a day. Most of the babies were delivered in the mothers' homes; most of the mothers, I discovered, were black and lived in slums. Two of us went out on call—one to administer ether, the other to deliver the baby. Were we all sound asleep in those years? It never occurred to me, or to any of my medical school colleagues, that this academic use of the poor was unconscionable: medical students acting as doctors, primitive anesthesia, unsanitary conditions.

That fall a show of female impersonators came to Cleveland. At the frat house I had joined in the general snickering and laughter caused by the mere mention of men dressing up as women. But I took a night off and went to see the show, hoping to meet other homosexuals.

I picked a corner table in the downtown bar where the show was playing, and as I listened to the begowned men sing their songs, I took in the audience. The crowd was as straight as they come: hand-holding married couples and dating couples having the hee-haw time of their lives. But if they were oafish in their way, so was I in mine. After the show, I went up to the master of ceremonies, who I assumed was gay, and, summoning up all my courage, said: "I'm homosexual, and I don't know any others, and I wonder if you could tell me where I could meet some." He stared at me as if I were very big to be still such a baby, and then he laughed. "Well, you can meet me," he said. "I'm one. But I'll tell you something, coming to a show like this is not a good way to meet men. You've seen our audience, haven't you?" Amused by my ignorance, he said he would take me to a gay bar as soon as he freshened up.

The front section of the bar we went to was straight; the back was packed with gay men. I remember asking my guide in astonishment if these were all homosexuals. "If they weren't," he said, "they wouldn't be back here." Innocent young doctor-to-be that I was, I wanted to walk around the room introducing myself to each of them. We will all be close friends, I thought.

My guide went to speak to a friend, leaving me to fend for myself. I walked up to the bar, still incredulous that there could be so many others like me, and ordered a beer. Soon I was talking to a young man—the third homosexual, I quickly told him, that I had ever talked to. He was amused. A few beers later he invited me to spend the night with him. Not having touched a man since Frank and I had broken up, I was too excited to flinch when, on our way to his place, he told me that he was a hairdresser. That night was all sex and no talk. The next morning his mother served us breakfast in the kitchen. What went through her mind I'll never know. Did she suspect? Did she know? Did she know and refuse to believe? I saw her son two more times and then dropped him; we had nothing in common. Also, I was afraid of being seen with a hair-dresser. And his casual acceptance of his nature irked me. Couldn't he at least *try* to pass in the straight world?

For the next ten years—until 1957—I continued to visit gay bars: in Cleveland, where I put in a year as an interne; in Detroit, to which I moved in 1950; and in New York City, to which I fled in 1954 to become one of that relatively free city's anonymous millions.

There were probably no more than two or three gay bars in either Cleveland or Detroit in the late forties and early fifties. Full of new faces on weekends, they were pretty empty on workday nights when only the regulars dropped in. For them the bar was a social club, a second home, the only place in town where they could relax. I had neither the time nor the money to become a regular when I was living in the Midwest. Then, too, I was going to be cured of my homosexuality by psychoanalysis. Should a recuperating fairy go to gay bars? Still, at about ten o'clock on my rare free evenings I would become restless and long for companionship, for someone to make love with. And I would go to a gay bar.

Because of my hospital schedule, these forays usually took place on weekends, and usually I returned from them disappointed. On my first excursion into the world of gay bars I had been excited and then tremendously relieved to find a man I could both touch and have some feeling for. But I was to find that this was the exception, not the rule. The regulars clung together at one end of the bar; I sat

51

apart, staring into space, too timid to start up a conversation. The occasional pickup was not likely to give much pleasure. Every bit as frightened as I was, my partner would frequently refuse to give me his real name or address. We spoke guardedly—if at all—about what it felt like to be gay, and there was little enough affection in the sex we shared. Most of the young men I spent a night with I never wanted to see again. Like the hairdresser, they came from a different world; we had nothing in common but our need and our fear and our guilt. Would my life as a homosexual consist of nothing but these grim one-night stands? My suspicion that it would seemed to confirm that being homosexual was a fate to be avoided at any cost.

I moved to Detroit in 1950 to start analysis (the handful of analysts in Cleveland were booked solid), to do a three-year residency in internal medicine, and to work overtime to pay for my analysis. As part of my new-life regimen, I worked hard at getting interested in women. The girls and women I had dated ever since high school had not helped; now I tried visiting whorehouses. But my experiences there proved that I was not yet prepared to enter the heterosexual world.

Working at the United Auto Workers clinic, I heard stories about an attractive local girl who slept around. Uncharacteristically, I sought her out and dated her. We got along. After a while she moved into my small apartment. She was bright, tolerant, and eager to please me. My spirit was willing, but my body was not; nothing happened between us in bed. I was afraid to explain why. She moved out after two weeks.

Shortly thereafter I had a letter from Frank telling me that he and his lover were now living together. My luck too was turning—I had met a gay doctor who opened my eyes to the fact that there was, after all, an alternative to the one-night-stand gay-bar scene. That he was a doctor was, in itself, important to me; that he had established what appeared to be a stable relationship with another man was also encouraging. They had met in San Francisco and then, after a year, moved together to Detroit so that the doctor could take a residency. San Francisco, they told me, was as sexually liberated as Detroit was repressed. I had heard the same thing about New York City from a homosexual couple just back from a vacation there; they reported that there were fifty, perhaps a hundred, gay bars and gay restaurants in New York. And they told me about Fire Island. To a provincial Midwesterner, these reports from both coasts seemed incredible. The fruited plain was obviously no place to hang out my shingle—if, that is, I was as unalterably homosexual as I suspected I was. By the fall of 1953, I had pretty well made up my mind that when I finished my specialty training I would move to New York.

In November, however, a very lovely, very thoughtful woman fell in love with me. Following my psychiatrist's implicit orders, I had tried—failing again and again—to "avoid having sexual experiences with men." Yet in spite of these lapses, I continued to hope that I might change, that one night I might be able to perform with a woman and the next morning wake up "a real man." When Laura came into my life, I thought she would be the one to work this miracle. We had met in the medical library; I liked her and asked her to a couple of dances. And I had met and liked her family. Laura and I lived in the same neighborhood. I was twenty-eight; she was two years younger. I knew that it was time for me to marry, if I were ever going to marry, and that if I were courting her, which I certainly seemed to be doing, I should be more sexually aggressive. Because I could not be, I felt obliged to say something. Unable to tell Laura the truth—I was still not sure it *was* the truth—I said that I was afraid I was impotent. She was a devout Catholic; but she wanted to marry me so much she offered to sleep with me—that sort of sacrifice sounds fishy nowadays, but it really meant something then. We spent many nights together, but I could not respond to her sexually. Overcome with guilt—I felt that I was using her, and I knew that I was hurting her terribly—I broke up with her.

That spring I made a number of decisions. I would give up analysis and stop struggling to deny my homosexuality. When I moved to New York in the summer, I would stop dating women and find gay friends. More than anything I would try to establish a long-term relationship with a man I loved and respected. I would still have to conceal my sexual identity from society at large, but I would no longer refuse to admit it to myself, and I would never again hide it from men like me.

In New York I found a job—the UAW had recommended me to the officers of the Health Insurance Plan of New York City—but no friends. My sister and brother-in-law were the only people I knew in the whole city. I had to turn back to the gay bars to find companions.

Friends in Detroit had provided me with a classified list of more than fifty gay bars in New York: elegant bars, homely bars, dancing bars, and so on. Gradually I was able to transfer my social life from the bars to the apartments and town houses of the men I had met there. My circle of acquaintances expanded in no time.

But perhaps we should slip back into those bars for a moment—I've been in a lot of them; you may never enter one—so that I can introduce you to some of the men I encountered in them.

The gay bars of Cleveland and Detroit had been, as a rule, dark and pretty shabby. In the summer of 1954 I walked into the East 55—a gay bar that took its name from its location on East Fifty-fifth Street in Manhattan—and found myself in a very posh place indeed. Everybody was well dressed; there was a fancy pianist jazzing up the air, and the restaurant served excellent food. Could a bumpkin physician who was also somewhat fussy afford to be seen in such a place? He could.

I met Mark at the East 55 bar one freezing winter night. He said I was the first gay man he had met who had a graduate degree in anything. He, in turn, was the first gay man I had met who was interested in social causes. He was a graduate of the Wharton School of Finance and worked with a well-known liberal organization. Something of a *nouveau demi-riche,* I had rented a small penthouse on East Fifty-second Street overlooking the river and the United Nations Building. I invited him up, and we talked for hours. We did not go to bed together. Homosexuals can be just friends, too. Mark and I still are.

Meeting Mark—and meeting him, moreover, in a gay bar—helped me to see gay social life in a new way. I had learned that there were places a homosexual could go where it was even possible to meet his peers.

The Blue Parrot—a couple of blocks from my apartment—was smaller, more intimate, decidedly less elegant, and cheaper than the East 55. Since it was so close to home, I often dropped in. The men who hung out there reminded me of my fraternity brothers back at Hiram, getting on and growing chunky. Mark, like most of the men at the East 55, wore elegantly tailored suits. The guys at the Blue Parrot dressed casually and looked straight.

It was at the Blue Parrot that I ran into Eric, though I tried to slip out before he spotted me. Eric was a doctor on the staff of the hospital at which I worked. He could not be gay, I thought; he was married, or anyway had been, and even had children. But he said hello before I could pay up and take off. I cringed. This was the first time I had met anyone in a gay bar whom I knew professionally. He would talk, and I would be through.

I had already concocted a cover story in case something like this ever happened: I was new to New York; I lived in the neighborhood; I didn't know what I was getting into— "We don't have bars like this back home"—I was just on my way out; and so on. Eric didn't pay much attention to my fast talk. He switched the conversation to hospital affairs. As he spoke, I noticed a man at the bar glancing at him and smiling. Then I recalled that I had seen them come in together. I had been too anxious to put one and one together. Suddenly Eric dropped hospital affairs and called down the bar, "Why don't you join us, Joe?" Joe came over, and Eric introduced him to me as his lover.

This was welcome news on two counts. Word about me would not get around, and I would have somebody to talk to at the hospital.

Joe was an architect whom Eric had met shortly after his divorce; they had immediately moved in together. At dinner the next night, I learned that Eric was involved in civil rights health causes. The three of us have been friends for twenty years now. Their relationship has lasted twenty-five years so far—almost five times as long as Eric's relationship with his wife. Eric and I made a point of introducing each other to the gay doctors we came to know— which not only made our working lives easier, but also enlarged our social lives.

Shaw's—also in my neighborhood, at Third Avenue and Forty-ninth Street—was a gay bar for a special set: the supermasculine crowd. The men who frequented Shaw's dressed up as city cowboys, in Levi's and boots and as much leather (such bars are known as leather bars) as they could pack onto one body. I looked almost criminally out of place in my blue business suit. I had come in part because I was intrigued by the thought of men who took such extreme measures to avoid effeminacy (no transvestite would have dared to enter Shaw's), but mainly to make a pickup.

I was leaning against a wall, drinking a beer and trying to look at ease, when incredible Steve marched in. I stared; everyone stared. To grasp the mood in that room then, the straight reader will have to imagine Jayne Mansfield in a tight halter top entering a crowded singles bar. But a famous actress would never enter a public place alone, nor would her arrival necessarily mean that she was looking for a partner for the night. Steve was tall, big-chested, with the biceps of an assiduous weight lifter. He did not even stop to order a drink; he just walked back and forth, as if he couldn't stand the thought of being cooped up in that bar. He looked about my age—thirty.

I had ample opportunity to admire him. Then all of a sudden he paused in front of me. Shy though I was, I asked if he wanted to get out of there and have a drink with me at my apartment. Even for a place like Shaw's this was a direct approach, and for me it was incredibly direct. But it worked. He seemed relieved at the prospect of escape; he smiled and said, "Let's go." And so, meek, mild-mannered Dr. Brown, astonished at his good fortune, walked out with Mr. Supermansfield.

Out on the street I asked him why he had agreed to come back with me. He said that he didn't like all that smoke in the bar, and that he couldn't stand the bars anyway. (Weeks later he told me that he had liked my smile, which must have been largely a nervous twitch.) I was tense as we set off together; I wondered how I could ever have interested—and how I could ever please—this colossus, and at the same time I anticipated the sexual pleasure the night could bring. But by the time we reached my apartment we were talking easily.

Would he like a drink? He asked for a glass of milk. I had a beer. This superman was a bit mystifying. In bed he proved to be affectionate and hungry for affection, content to talk and kiss and caress, reluctant to go any further. If he had inhibitions, so had I, and many nights were to pass before we were sufficiently at ease with each other and with ourselves to overcome them.

I had imagined that we would spend one intensely and exclusively sexual night together. The fact is that Steve and I were lovers for nearly a year. He had depths that his muscular façade belied—which is, perhaps, only a fancy way of saying that he was as neurotic as I was. He was a homosexual dreamboat who had had a particularly terrible time coming to terms with his homosexuality. He had grown up fatherless, and he had grown up poor. He was not very bright; he had just managed to graduate from high school. And as a clerk in a department store he felt trapped on a low rung of the social ladder. As if to inflate his ego, he had built up his body with a passion. At the same time, he resented being pursued for his body alone. After we had been lovers for a time, he told me that he had opened up with me on our walk home from Shaw's that night because I seemed to regard him as a person and not just as a sex object. I like to think I did.

Looking at Steve's body helped me to silence those childhood banshees who still cried in my ears, "Fairies are sissies." And his craving for affection and approval made me, for once, feel needed. Frank, with his happy childhood, had had little understanding or sympathy for the sense of inadequacy that haunted me. Fused only by the experience of discovering our homosexuality together, we had remained emotionally estranged. He had said he loved me, but he had never said he needed me.

And it was wonderful to feel needed.

Steve and I took a long trip in the summer of 1955. We visited my parents—surely no one in Ravenna, Ohio, suspected that Superman was gay—drove up to Detroit, and then camped out in Canada. I was happy to get out of the city and be alone with Steve. In New York our different ideas of what our social life as a couple should be created a problem, as did my having been promoted and twice given substantial raises while Steve's job and modest salary remained the same. Moreover, I was becoming aware that although Steve didn't want to be loved for his body alone, he really didn't have that much else to offer.

Steve's idea of our social life was just the two of us and a few good friends, mostly his. I, on the other hand, wanted to create the gay equivalent of the life I would have lived as a straight doctor in the Midwest. In my first year in New York I had met many stimulating, successful, and apparently well-adjusted homosexual men, and I wanted to get to know many of them as friends and to entertain them often. Steve took this to mean that he wasn't enough for me, that I considered him inadequate. And, as a matter of fact, he did not have much to say to the people I was meeting. He grew increasingly hostile toward them and surly toward me. Eventually we broke up. I don't know whether our relationship helped him, but it certainly helped me. Living with Steve for eleven months, and loving him nearly all of that time, was the first real evidence I had that homosexual life had more to offer me than a string of superficial encounters.

My visits to gay bars tapered off as I gradually put together a community of physicians, lawyers, teachers, actors —men or friends of men I had met at gay bars, at work, or simply in the neighborhood. We all gave parties. We made up a circle within which we found affection and release from anxiety. I began to feel at home in my skin, with my life.

Not all homosexual men are able to make this transition. Some men I met at gay bars in the fifties can still be found in them. Others, discouraged in their attempts to find partners in bars or on the street, have buried themselves in their work, totally repressing their sexual urges, like the

Chicago executive whose letter I quoted. A few married and tried to become family men. I have lost touch with the ones whose marriages appeared to be working out. Those whose marriages merely endure are apt to resort to Turkish baths, to male prostitutes, or to public lavatories whose stinking stalls serve as bedrooms. The men driven to engage in sexual acts in public places are the most vulnerable to arrest. And it is the disgrace that accompanies arrest that impels many to suicide. In the summer of 1972 a married psychiatrist, arrested in a public lavatory, took a fatal overdose of sleeping pills. In 1968 a young interne from a small Southern town was arrested in a police raid on a Turkish bath in Manhattan; the next day, panicked that word would get back to his family, he shot himself. I had met this boy at a party a few months before. Assuming he would break through and find friends, I did not ask him, as I now do ask young homosexual doctors, if I could help in any way. In the past we all assumed that the search for a meaningful gay life had to be a lonely one.

But times have changed. With the help of the gay activist groups, young homosexual men today are much more able than my generation to find companionship, advice, and—in some cases—a cause to fight for.

Francis is a twenty-eight-year-old gay activist who speaks on homosexuality at high schools and colleges in and around New York City, writes for *Advocate*, a national gay magazine, and is a poet and playwright. He is short, thin, shy; he wears glasses and appears—is, in fact—rather scholarly. Yet one senses that he is inwardly strong, a young man who has made up his mind on important issues and will stand firm.

Francis grew up in the West. His father was a construction foreman who believed, Francis says, that "being mechanically gifted was the essence of manhood." Francis was a lousy mechanic, and just as wretched at sports as I was. His father, whom Francis characterizes as taciturn, rigid, and forbidding, didn't know what to make of him. During the Depression his father had been a miner and very left-wing, but in 1964 he was a Democrat for Goldwater, and in 1968 he voted for Nixon. Francis's mother was cheerful and vital. Both parents were strict with him, as his older sister had been "too wild."

A flop both as a mechanic and as a jock, Francis attempted to prove himself through scouting—he became an Eagle Scout—and church work. His parents had not been religious; he got them interested in religion. He planned to become a Baptist minister, but college changed all that. He marched in antiwar demonstrations, joined Students for a Democratic Society to protest the war more effectively, and abandoned religion. He had become "the kind of person my parents had warned me about."

In 1968 Francis had hoped the Democratic party would come up with a program to alter American society radically. But the platform adopted by the party disappointed him, and the campaign left him feeling completely betrayed. Traditional forms of political action, he came to believe, led nowhere. And yet he could not align himself with the Communist party or with the Socialist Worker's party wing of the SDS. He left the Democratic party, extricated himself from SDS, and, when his draft board called him up, became a conscientious objector.

Francis's radical friends had advised him to "fag out"— to tell his draft board that he was homosexual and thus be classified as psychologically unfit for service. But in 1968 he did not consider himself to be homosexual, and he objected to this stratagem as being an easy way out.

As an adolescent Francis had had sexual relations with both boys and girls. In graduate school, at Bennington College in Vermont, he had lived with a woman. Even so, he felt that something was wrong with him sexually. He saw several psychiatrists, one—and only one—of whom suggested that perhaps he was homosexual. Francis had not seriously considered this as a possibility, despite the fact that his dreams and fantasies were always and only about men. Like so many of us, he simply could not believe that he was "one of those." But the painful crumbling of his affair with the Bennington woman left him convinced of his homosexuality. He knew nothing about how homosexuals could live; he knew only that he had failed with women and that he did not want to hurt another woman. He decided to lead a celibate life. Ironically, the alternative service job to which he was assigned shortly after deciding to be chaste was with the Planned Parenthood Association in New York.

The Stonewall riots of 1969 erupted soon after Francis moved to New York. Just as college and the SDS had forced him to revise his middle-class values, so now the gay activist movement forced him to think about what kind of moral revolution America needed. Yet when he spoke with his radical friends about sexual issues, he found them to be as conservative in regard to women's liberation and homosexual civil rights as his parents had been in regard to the Vietnam war. At Bennington, Francis had become a feminist; in New York, he became a gay activist. The gay movement gave him the moral basis he needed to acknowledge and accept his sexual nature. "I am what I am," Francis told me. "I'll only be doing damage to myself and others if I deny it. I accept my nature and take pride in it as other men and women do in theirs. And I intend to fight for my right to live and love as I wish and for the rights of men and women like me."

Through the gay activist movement, Francis met a number of young men as socially concerned as he. He made friends, renounced his vow of chastity, and found lovers.

To the heterosexual reader, this possibly happy ending will no doubt seem less dramatic than it is. The heterosexual, of course, has never had to struggle very seriously with the moral issues involved in accepting his or her sexual identity. When, I wonder, did he last ask himself whether it was right to make love for sheer pleasure instead of for the sole, theologically justified purpose of procreation? The maxim that the majority is always right —no matter how many philosophers have blasted it—is still backed up by law. For the sexual minority to which I belong, the struggle has been only too painfully real and long. And for a young man like Francis—after traveling the circuitous route from religion through politics to feminism—to finally find a moral sanction for his sexuality represents a considerable achievement. A minority happy ending, if you will.

The Gay Activists Alliance of New Jersey meets in a church—a Unitarian church—in Hackensack. How different the atmosphere there is from the dives that homosexual men of my era slunk into! In January 1974, three months after I came out publicly, I was invited to speak at one of their weekly evening meetings. I had attended meetings of young activists in Manhattan, but this would be my first trip to the sticks. It proved full of surprises.

I was driven to New Jersey by a straight-looking banker —complete with blue suit, red-striped tie, flesh-colored glasses, resonant businessman's voice—and his lover with whom he had been living for twelve years. Our first stop was at the home of a schoolteacher, who served a buffet for the GAA officers. The teacher and his lover opened the door on a scene that reminded me of every church social I had attended as a kid: men and women milling around the table—casseroles long on noodles and short on meat, a big tossed salad, cakes. Homosexual men, in couples; homosexual women, in couples. This was a very different scene from the one I had become accustomed to in New York. It was folksy; the group was sexually integrated and included people from a wide range of professions. While I was talking with a lesbian accountant, a young mechanic with a huge mop of hair walked over and asked her if she could help him with the books of a garage he was planning to open. The mechanic, I soon learned, was the president of the New Jersey GAA.

At the meeting in the church I was surprised to find even greater diversity in profession and age (from eighteen to around sixty). I saw men in leather and men in frills, men in suits and men in casual wear, women in skirts and women in jeans. The fifty or sixty people made as much happy noise as any church group gathered for a social.

A brief business meeting was held before I spoke, in which the program for the coming months was announced: dances, picnics, an evening at a skating rink. Then people were allowed to make two-minute personal announcements: an apartment needed, a couple's anniversary, the opening of a new business (would members kindly patronize it?). My speech was followed by a social hour, which included dancing—men with men, women with women, naturally. I didn't dance that night. Instead, I talked—with, among other people, a middle-aged priest, a high school boy, and a college senior.

The priest—dressed in sport shirt, slacks, loafers—told me that he was one of the founders of Dignity, a gay Catholic organization, and that he had come out publicly, at least to the extent of attending these meetings regularly. Later, the high school boy approached me. He said he was thinking of consulting a psychiatrist. I asked him why. Because he had just broken up with a boy he had been going with, he said, and he was afraid he might never have another long-term relationship. I asked him if he thought boys and girls his age—he had just turned eighteen—were ready for marriage, and if he thought they should go into analysis if they were not. He stopped to think that one over. I then introduced him to one of the high school teachers, a man better able to counsel him than I. The teacher, in turn, introduced me to a young man who said that he was going to medical school and that I was partly responsible for his decision. When he discovered that he was homosexual, he had given up his dream of becoming a doctor because he had thought homosexuals could never enter that profession. (Myths like this fester where people are afraid or too isolated to ask questions.) After reading about me, he had determined to go ahead.

That night as I drifted off to sleep I thought of my great-uncle who had been a general practitioner in Hebron, Ohio, and whom I had often accompanied on house calls. He had known the town banker, the mechanic, the teachers, the men and women who ran the stores and shops. Now I was meeting homosexuals just like them, in the same small-town atmosphere. I felt at home with them. My great-uncle, dead for many years now, was a wonderful man, but he would have been shocked and disturbed by these young people.

Later that month I spoke at a gay function at the State University of New York at Albany. If the Hackensack experience reminded me of the pleasant evenings I had once spent in a Methodist church basement, the trip to Albany made me wistfully aware of how joyless my college years had been.

I was introduced to the large group of homosexual students of both sexes by Joe Norton, a thin, white-haired professor who had come out first on campus and then on local television in 1973. Professor Norton is a grandfather —stereotypists, take note—who discovered his homosexuality in his middle fifties and divorced his wife of many years. He had been one of the most beloved figures on campus, I was told, and he remained so after his announcement. As he proceeded with his introductory comments, I thought: This is exactly what was missing at Hiram and at Western Reserve—an older man I could really talk to.

After my speech, a group of students escorted me across the campus to the hall where a dance was to be held. It was snowing. The campus with its slopes and hills and trees reminded me in its beauty of Hiram. In both high school and college I had always looked forward to the annual Christmas dance, hoping against hope that I would feel something for the girl I took, that something would finally click. Nothing ever did, of course. But these Albany students would have those memories of college days that previously had been reserved for heterosexuals.

The lights were low in the hall. Through the huge windows I looked out at the trees fixed by the falling snow. Several students asked me to dance. I did the best I could —a forties jitterbug to rock. When the music slowed down, I asked a shy young man to dance. He was the secretary of the gay student group, it turned out, and I was the first person who had ever asked him to dance. I had danced in gay bars, but it was nothing like this. There I had felt a combination of alienation and defiance, as if dancing with a man was a deed that divided me from the rest of the world. Here I felt part of the student community, part of a tradition. At the age of forty-nine, I felt like a student— for the first time in my life.

I danced and talked until four in the morning. The last young man I talked to was the president of the gay group. He looked the sort of affable jock who would have been elected president of a fraternity back in my college days. With men like him and Professor Norton around and "out," the young homosexual student would certainly not confuse homosexuality with effeminacy as I and too many others had done.

Two months later I heard that this young man's parents

had reacted in the classic manner to his open avowal of his sexual identity: They had disowned him. He had had to leave school and was now unloading boats on the Albany docks.

# CHAPTER FIVE

# Parents

I did not tell my parents that I was homosexual. Nor did most homosexual men of my generation tell their parents. We excused our reticence with the thought that we were sparing them the agony of having to think about us as sexual beings—or, to put it another way, of having to understand us. On the surface, this policy had its advantages: We did not put our parents in the extreme position of having to decide whether to accept us or reject us. The disadvantage was the distance our silence put between us and our parents, so that invariably we emerged from the years-long process of discovering our sexual identity feeling estranged from them. We had not felt free to turn to them when we needed them the most; we had not been able to share with them our relief when we came to accept ourselves or our joy when we found a man we loved. Instead, we shared with them a version of our lives from which all the essential passages had been expurgated.

Concealment is still the policy followed by most homosexual men. In the main, it is the young who confront their parents with the truth, particularly the young activists, because they believe their parents should know and because, given the public nature of the activists' work, their parents are likely to find out anyway. The few apolitical homosexual sons who tell their parents either have been accustomed to talking openly with them or have decided that a relationship that must gloss over such a major part of their lives is not worth maintaining.

As a rule, parents find it no less difficult to accept homosexuality than does their son, although, of course, the gay son feels and is alone, while his parents have society's tacit support for their way of living and loving. And just as most homosexuals go through a prolonged period of disbelief and denial, so, too, do many parents, some of whom take the ultimate step of disowning their son—"If you're queer, you're no son of mine." Every year hundreds of disowned or runaway homosexual adolescents turn up at the office of the National Gay Task Force in New York City, looking for food, shelter, jobs; hundreds more roam the streets, keeping themselves alive by working as male prostitutes.

It takes some parents years to adjust to their son's confession. A few accept fully and without hesitation, out of simple love or a deeper understanding of human sexuality than that of society as a whole. I think, in this respect, of the letter Freud wrote in 1935 to an American woman whose son was homosexual—a letter that expresses a humane insight the American Psychiatric Association officially came to acknowledge only in 1973:

Dear Mrs. X,

I gather from your letter that your son is a homosexual. I am most impressed by the fact that you do not mention this term yourself in your information about him. May I question you, why do you avoid it? Homosexuality is assuredly no advantage, but it is nothing to be ashamed of, no vice, no degradation, it cannot be classified as an illness. . . .*

* *American Journal of Psychiatry*, Vol. 107 (April 1951), as reprinted in *The Problem of Homosexuality in Modern Society*, Hendrik M. Ruitenbeek, ed. (New York: E. P. Dutton, 1963), p. 1.

In the following pages several homosexual men describe how they came to tell their parents of their homosexuality and how their parents reacted. And some parents describe how it felt to discover that they had a homosexual son, though it was not easy for me to talk in depth with parents of homosexuals. I could approach only those who had accepted their sons' homosexuality, since the others would doubtless have refused to see me. Also, as the parents of many homosexual men of my generation are not aware that their sons are homosexual, I have had to turn to the parents of younger friends and acquaintances. Even these accepting parents, willing to talk about their reactions to their sons' coming out, find it difficult to express themselves in anything but very general terms. This is partly because they have never been able to talk about their experience with other people, even close relatives, and partly because it is something they would prefer not to be reminded of. It may be, too, that parents of a homosexual son are no more at ease with me than I am with them; both sides are involved in something very new—speaking openly about homosexuality.

I would like to deal at the start with one aspect of parental relations with homosexual sons: Most parents are exceedingly slow to perceive (or to admit to themselves) that their son is homosexual, despite abundant evidence that he is. I shall narrow my focus here to adult homosexual men in long-term relationships, men who presumably have established households and found a place in the gay community. It follows that the social as well as the private lives they lead differ significantly from those of straight men. One would expect that parents would draw conclusions from these very visible differences. Why are they so slow to do so?

Undoubtedly, like most of the older generation and many of the younger, parents accept the stereotype of the homosexual man; thus, if their son is not effeminate, he cannot be homosexual. Parents of a homosexual son are also apt to suffer from a kind of psychic blindness, simply screening out what they do not wish to see. On the other hand, in some instances at least, what homosexual men take to be parental blindness may merely be discretion. Confused or ashamed, the parents take care not to betray what they have perceived. The parents of many of my middle-aged homosexual friends have never given up asking, "When are you going to get married?" They have never asked their sons if they are homosexual. Occasionally a widowed parent has moved in with the son and the son's lover, without ever giving any indication that he or she understands the relationship between the two men. As I say, it is difficult to know where blindness ends and where what older people consider to be tactfulness begins.

A number of young homosexuals refuse to make even the slightest effort to conceal their homosexuality from their parents but, rather, leave it up to them to raise the issue. "I'd always told my parents the truth about anything I was doing," a Princeton student told me, "so when I realized I was gay I decided I would answer any question they asked about it. My mother never put much together and never got much. She asked me if I was going to get married, and I said no. She asked me if I wanted a family, and I said no. That's as far as she took it. My father was more concerned. He took me out one night for a long talk. He began by confessing that he could never sleep with a black woman and he didn't know why he had that hangup. He wanted to know if I thought he was a racist. I said no. Then, *finally*, he said, well, how about men? Do you think you could sleep with a man? I said, yes, I could. He said he didn't think he could at all. Of course, I expected him to take the question one step further, but he didn't. Both my mother and father have met my lover—they've met him

71

hundreds of times—and yet they've never asked me a single question. My mother doesn't really understand it or, as far as I can tell, even think about it. But I'm sure my father knows. He just doesn't want to ask so he won't ever have to hear me say, 'Yes, it's true.' And I must say I have no great compulsion to tell him. If he doesn't want to hear it, I don't know why I should bother to sit down and say it, word by word."

Telling his parents is one of the most emotional and significant events in the life of a homosexual man. It is, perhaps, at least in our society now, the ultimate test of love, both for the parents and their son.

Gerald, a thirty-one-year-old white from a conservative Irish-American family, and Bill, a twenty-five-year-old black from Mississippi, have been living together monogamously as lovers in New York City for three years. They jointly own and run an antique shop, and Gerald is a free-lance illustrator. Bill is a devout Baptist; Gerald, raised Catholic, considers himself religious but does not go to church. Bill had had only one lover before Gerald; Gerald had had a seven-year relationship with another man. In the summer of 1974 they told their respective parents that they were homosexual.

Gerald and his mother first tentatively broached the subject of his homosexuality in 1967, when he was studying theater in graduate school. His mother, Gerald says, describes that conversation as "an attempt to reach out"— an attempt that failed, he adds, "because of her choice of words. She said that one had to be wary of the kind of people one met in the theater world, that it attracted a lot of queers. I withdrew completely. I was still in the process of acknowledging my homosexuality, and I just was not ready to talk about it, especially with someone who used words like that. I was horrified that she suspected I was gay, and I put an end to the conversation by saying that there were homosexual people in all walks of life, not only in the theater, and that I knew what I was doing and everything was okay."

Through Bill, Gerald learned "of the indignities and horrors the black man suffers in a predominantly white society" and came to perceive that he, too, belonged to a minority. "Then," Gerald said, "I began to wonder how I was going to confront society. Was I going to continue to be ashamed of being homosexual or was I going to stand up and just be what I was and let those around me adjust to it?"

A visit with his younger brother in the spring of 1974 pushed Gerald toward a decision. He and Bill drove out to an auction of antique furniture that was being held not far from Gerald's brother's weekend cottage. Gerald wanted to introduce Bill to at least one member of his family, and his brother, to whom he was close and who was a guidance counselor in a largely black elementary school in Manhattan, seemed the safest person to start with. Even so, Gerald was planning to introduce Bill not as his lover, but as his business partner.

As soon as the two men got out of their car, Gerald's brother's collies began to bark at them. The dogs chased them all the way to the door and continued to bark even after Gerald and Bill had sat down in the living room. Gerald asked why the dogs were so excited, and his brother replied, "You know why." When Gerald said he didn't, his brother told him, "Well, we don't see many like Bill around here."

"Our mouths just fell open," Gerald recalled. "Bill slipped out of the house. Later he said he had felt like walking all the way back to Manhattan. I told my brother that his remark was stupid, unbelievable. He protested that he hadn't meant it that way, that his dogs weren't used to seeing black people, that was all. I walked out, and Bill and I drove off.

"When I went home for my thirty-first birthday I got to talking about the incident with my father, who is a retired taxi driver. He kept insisting that my brother hadn't meant any offense and I was just being hypersensitive.

"I said I felt that I couldn't bring Bill home, that someone might say something unintentionally, but that I wanted to bring him home because, well, he was my business partner. My mother said, 'Oh, we don't mind.' But I wasn't asking if they *minded*. I was telling them that as my partner he was due a certain amount of respect. Then my father said, 'You're not going to bring him around here, are you?' and I said, 'I just can't cope with that kind of thinking. I can't even understand it.'

"That night everything came to a head. I remember saying, 'You don't want me here. You don't want my life in this house.' I had to bite my tongue to keep from crying. I don't cry easily. I'd been brought up not to.

"As I said good-bye I hugged my father and kissed my mother. I didn't want them to think we were parting on bad terms. But I left that house feeling I could never see them again."

That night Gerald wrote a letter to his mother—"I was afraid my father wouldn't be able to take this blow to his male ego, so I told her to keep the letter to herself"—in which he announced that he was homosexual and offered to withdraw from the family if his parents could not respect the depth of his feelings for Bill:

When I come out to the house I come as the person the family expects me to be rather than as the person I really am. I watch my brothers and their wives holding hands and hugging while I sit, like some loveless clown, trying to answer ridiculous questions about when I'm going to get married. . . .

... you needn't feel any shame—the test of your parenthood is not what your son's sexual preference is but what kind of human being you have raised. You and dad have never "failed" me in any way. And now I realize that my being a homosexual does not mean that I have failed you. The trouble with most people is that they feel they have to take a stand on anything that is different from them—they make it better or worse, judge it. Whites see blacks as not only different but inferior. Which is also the way heterosexuals see homosexuals. Behind it all is fear.

The first thing Gerald's mother did was show the letter to her husband, from whom, she later explained to Gerald, she had never kept anything secret. Both were upset, but less by Gerald's announcement (his mother had long suspected that he was a homosexual) than by his having thought they would not want to see him again. They immediately telephoned him to say how much they both loved him. And that night Gerald's mother wrote to him.

Dear Gerry,
Your letter made me feel very sad. Not because I am ashamed of the fact you are a homosexual, but because you did not have faith enough in us to talk this over instead of allowing "this wall" you refer to to be built up between us. Don't you think your world would have been a better place if you had allowed us to help guide you in some way? What ever can have made you feel we couldn't understand something you had no control over to begin with? You say you fear what we will think of you. You should know by now that we love you very much and that your fears have always been our fears. Gerry, we respect you, we think the world of you. I know what a terrible burden this has been for you. I'm glad it's over. I'm just sorry you felt you had to wait so long to talk to us about it. . . .

Gerald was soon to discover that although his parents accept him, they do not really understand his relationship with Bill. His father cannot comprehend how a man can love and enjoy sex with another man; his mother still regards Bill as Gerald's sex companion and possibly his friend, but nothing more. He is still wary of introducing Bill to them, but on the whole he is pleased with the new openness. "I'm more comfortable with my parents now than I've ever been. If I had trusted them more, perhaps we wouldn't have lost so much time in getting to know each other. As it is, I'm thirty-one, my mother's fifty-nine, and my father's sixty-one, and we're just getting started."

A few weeks after Gerald wrote to his mother, Bill decided to go home to Mississippi to tell his parents (his father works at a textile plant, his mother is a practical nurse). "I've always been very close to my family, and it hurt to keep this secret from them," Bill explained. "I called to say I was coming home to tell them something very serious. I expected them to drum me out of the family. I spent a week preparing a speech. But then I got home and my mother was sitting on the couch across from me, and I just blurted it all out.

"I knew it wasn't going to be easy for her—I grew up with a lot of macho types—and it wasn't. She cried and I cried. I reminded her that she had taught me to be proud of myself as a black man, and I told her that I had had to learn for myself to be proud as a gay man. She guessed she understood that, but she cried anyway. She cried that I had lost my manhood. I tried to explain to her that homosexuality has got nothing to do with manhood. And I could see she was beginning to understand that I hadn't lost my manhood. She became very tender with me and threw her arms around me and said, 'And you went through all this all by yourself.'

"Then I told my father, who's very masculine, the master of the family in every way. He didn't know what homosexuality was. He didn't even know the meaning of the word. But in the end his love for me as a son proved out.

He decided that since he knew me first as his son and loved me and that since I was no different now that he knew I was a homosexual, nothing had really changed, at least his love for me hadn't. I think that because of all the things he had gone through as a black man, he could understand what I had had to go through as a homosexual. After I was finished, he said, 'Why didn't you come to us? How could you go through this all alone? Why didn't you come sooner?' And I said, 'Daddy, when I was younger and I couldn't drive mules or pick cotton as fast as my brother, you were always at me. So how could I ever come to you about this?"

The only member of Bill's family who could not accept him was his older brother, whom Bill describes as "a very macho black man." His brother recently told him that when an old girl friend of Bill's had asked how he was getting on in New York, he thought of telling her that Bill had turned out not to be a man. "I'm ashamed of you," he said. "Then tell people that I died," Bill answered. Later, his nineteen-year-old sister consoled him by saying: "I'm a part of you, Bill, and I can never be ashamed of you. It would be like being ashamed of myself."

Since then, Bill and Gerald have visited Bill's family together. "Even my brother likes Gerald," Bill told me. "Telling my family was one of the best things I ever did. I wanted them to know about me, and now they do. My family proved out—even my brother may turn around."

John is seventeen. His divorced mother, a waitress, caught him having sex with another boy when he was eleven. Becoming quite irrational, she beat him, called him a "fucking fag," and told him to get out of the house. Since then, he has kept himself alive by taking odd jobs and by hustling on the streets of New York. Occasionally he returns to visit his mother, whom he both loves and fears. She never receives him without some taunt about his homosexuality: "If you want to put on makeup and wear some of my clothes, it's all right, we'll be sisters," or, once when John brought her a bouquet, "I don't want flowers from a fag," or, "Why don't you suck some cunt instead of some cock? It would make a man out of you." She is always telling John he should enlist in the Army—which as a homosexual he cannot do—because it would make a man out of him.

By now John prefers hustling to working, because "I earn more money from hustling and some of the men give me affection, and I can use that too. My mother makes me feel that everything I've ever done is wrong."

William was forty-three years old when he joined the National Gay Task Force in 1973. Subsequently he invited a number of television and show business personalities to a cocktail party in order to acquaint them with the aims of the gay movement. Whereupon he was promptly disinherited by his mother, a famous actress who has worked closely with many homosexual men. The curious thing was that she had known for some years that William was homosexual. Throughout the 1960's William had pretended to her that he spent his evenings with a series of women. One night his mother cross-examined him about these invented women and got him to admit that it was men he was dating. Her comment, reminiscent of Senator Joseph McCarthy's famous "That's the most unheard of thing I ever heard of," was: "I don't care if you tell me lies as long as you tell me the truth." William was understandably bewildered by this, but he continued to maintain superficially amicable relations with his mother; he continued to help her arrange, and also to attend, her many cocktail and dinner parties, which featured assorted presidents of the United States, their wives, and secretaries of state. William's mother takes status very seriously; only when her son attempted to link celebrities with the gay cause did she explode. She must have regarded his inviting them as a raid on her domain, and his being openly gay with them as a threat to her own status. She went through the list of invited guests and called them up, one by one, seeking to dissuade them from attending her son's party. When she failed, she accused him of willfully spoiling her life. "Why couldn't you have waited to come out until after I was dead?" she cried.

Tim's parents may seem more like situation-comedy parents than like real people, so Archie Bunkeresque are their reactions. There is probably some distortion at work here; I am, after all, using Tim's account. On the other hand, the whole subject of homosexuality has for so long been dealt with in clichés that people, particularly troubled parents, find it difficult to relinquish them. Grasping at clichés precludes thought; it is a buffer against reality.

Tim grew up in a Jewish neighborhood in Brooklyn. His father and mother—a fifty-three-year-old businessman and a fifty-year-old clerk-typist—were strongly prejudiced against blacks; Tim supported the black civil rights movement. His parents supported the war in Vietnam; Tim strongly opposed it. At their twenty-sixth wedding anniversary, his father proposed a toast to Tim's older brother, who was serving in Vietnam: "Thank God nobody in our family's been rejected by the Army. We don't have any fags in *this* family." Three years before, at thirteen, Tim had realized he was a homosexual. As he is in no way effeminate, his family naturally assumed he was straight.

In 1971, Tim's last year in college, he read about the Gay Activists Alliance and decided to attend a meeting. "I wanted to check out what kind of people went. I drove past the place twelve times, and when I saw that none of the guys who were going in were wearing lipstick or carrying a pocketbook, I went in."

The business of that night's meeting was to plan ways to assure that antidiscrimination legislation would be passed. Politics had always interested Tim. So had men. He joined the GAA on the spot, and that night, for the first time, he slept with a man. Two weeks later he moved to Greenwich Village—a move that prompted his predictable father to ask: "Why do you want to live there? That's where all the fags live." Tim replied that the reason was that he had found a cheap apartment. Within the GAA, Tim worked hard, and soon he became its chief lobbyist with the City Council.

Tim learned about discrimination during the next two years. After college he took a job as a social worker in Manhattan. He was fired after his supervisor saw him holding hands with a friend in a movie theater line. The following year he was fired from another social agency after appearing on television as an advocate of gay civil rights.

It was through this television show—a special newscast report on gay liberation—that Tim's parents discovered his homosexuality. He had not planned it that way. The report was shown only hours after it was filmed, and, caught up in the day's political activities, Tim realized too late that he should have spoken to his parents before they saw him on television. Perhaps, he thought, they would not watch the news that night, or perhaps the footage taken of him would not be used.

Tim's older brother, back from Vietnam, and his younger sister were watching a movie on television with their parents and grandmother when, during a program break, an announcer said that the news that night would include a special report on gay liberation. Tim's brother and sister were aware of his activities with the GAA. His brother had even attended a GAA meeting and had come all the way from urging Tim to see a psychiatrist to accepting and supporting him. As soon as the movie was over, Tim's brother tried to change the channel. But his parents wanted to see that special report. The program included shots of gay activists in three different parts of the city. Tim's brother recalls that during the first episode his father muttered: "The fags should be put in a boat and bombed." The last episode began with a shot of Tim declaring that there were twenty million homosexuals in America and that Mayor Lindsay had better come out strongly for gay civil rights before attempting to become President. Tim's brother said that their father's initial reaction was: "He was the first kid in the neighborhood to like niggers, the first kid to stop eating grapes, the first kid to come out against the Vietnam war, and now he's the first kid to support the queers. It's just a phase. He'll outgrow it." He could not believe that a son of his was a homosexual.

Before Tim's next visit home, for his sister's sweet sixteen party, his parents had questioned his brother and sister and concluded that they had "a fag in the family" after all. When he appeared at the party, his father remarked: "Son, if you want to be queer as a three-dollar bill, that's your business." Tim walked away without saying a word. Then his mother approached him. She put her arm around his shoulders. Tim took this to mean that she was going to accept him. "Tim," she said, "I've made only one mistake in my life." Tim asked her what she meant. "Twenty-two years ago," she said, "I should have had an abortion." Since then, Tim's mother has taken to telling neighbors and friends that he is dead. And Tim's father speaks to him as if he were a complete stranger when Tim calls to speak to his sister or brother.

Even for parents who are sympathetic, the process of acceptance of a homosexual son is likely to take many years. Immediate acceptance, when it is given, is usually more an official pronouncement—a declaration of good will—than an emotional fact. In order to truly accept homosexuality in a son, parents must learn to recognize and respect the depth of their son's love for another man. This kind of understanding requires meeting their son's friends, perhaps talking with other parents of homosexuals, and reading—although the reading list is, admittedly, a short one.

Mrs. Rae Kameny is the seventy-eight-year-old mother of the gay activist leader Frank Kameny. She was a widow in her early fifties when her son, who was then about thirty, told her that he was homosexual. He had just come out publicly in order to fight for gay civil rights.

Mrs. Kameny said that it took her a year or two to accept her son. In the beginning, she said, "I believed in the concept that there was something wrong with Frank, and I blamed myself. I had terrible guilt feelings, and I spent many sleepless nights wondering where I had gone wrong, what I had neglected to do."

Mrs. Kameny suggested to Frank that he see a psychiatrist. One of the first homosexual leaders to realize that the psychiatric establishment was appallingly ignorant on the subject of homosexuality, Frank was gradually able to convince his mother that there was no more reason for him to change his sexual preference than there was for her to blame herself. "He explained that what he was had nothing to do with his upbringing," Mrs. Kameny recalls, "and I've come to believe this, for I have a daughter who's a heterosexual, and the two of them were brought up in the same way in the same home. Little by little, through talking with my son and reading the books he gave me, I learned to accept that these things happen. I am now very proud of my son."

When she herself had accepted Frank's homosexuality,

Mrs. Kameny decided to tell one of her five brothers, the one to whom she felt the closest. "I thought I could confide in him. I couldn't have been more shocked at the way he took it. He was just simply livid. He fumed and he raved. He said, 'Don't you give him any money. Don't you help him. He's sick. I don't want to have anything to do with him.' This from a mature man whom I thought I could trust! And in all the years that have passed since then, he has never for a single moment accepted it."

Mrs. Kameny's advice to parents of homosexuals: "Accept them. Love them. *Show* them that you love them. And above all, don't blame yourselves."

Does the "blame" for homosexuality rest with the parents? Should parents feel guilty because they have produced a homosexual son? For years I believed that the answer to both questions was yes. Reading self-appointed psychiatric authorities on homosexuality, I could see, only too clearly, that my parents fit the stereotype of those who allegedly produce homosexual sons.

The psychoanalyst Dr. Irving Bieber was one authority whose views I took seriously. In *Homosexuality*, Dr. Bieber postulated that the most common situation producing a homosexual was a hostile or withdrawn father and a close-binding mother.* Ostensibly, my family seemed to substantiate Dr. Bieber's hypothesis. My father had withdrawn from me and later had been hostile toward me; and my mother had adored me. It took me a while to see that there were some serious flaws in this sort of reasoning.

First, my father did not begin to withdraw from me until I was nine. This was during the Depression, when he was obliged to do work he felt was far beneath him. Experts agree that sexual preference is formed very early—certainly by the age of five or six; some would say by the

* Irving Bieber, *Homosexuality* (New York: Basic Books), 1962.

83

age of three or four—and my father and I got along very well in those years of my life. He rejected me—partly because he was disappointed in his own life and partly because I had failed to measure up as an athlete—when my sexual preference had long been set.

Nor did my relations with my mother really fit Dr. Bieber's stereotype. The only sense in which she could be said to resemble the close-binding or seductive mother he had described was that she was warm and loving. She did not do many of the things mothers of homosexual sons are supposed to do. She did not try to dissuade me from dating girls. Far from it—she encouraged me to date. She did not try to keep me from having close relationships with other people, and she did not urge me to help her with supposedly effeminate tasks, such as cooking. Also, if she was affectionate to me, she was equally affectionate to my sister, who is heterosexual and as free of neuroses as can be.

Looking outside my immediate family, I found additional evidence that Dr. Bieber's hypothesis was not generally applicable. My mother had three sisters, all very like her in personality, all with absent or ineffectual husbands, and all with sons, none of whom became homosexual.

Dr. Bieber based his hypothesis on studies made not of well-adjusted homosexuals, but of homosexuals in therapy. Not surprisingly, he found that they came from troubled homes. Thus, of the 106 homosexuals he studied, seventy-nine had fathers who were classified as detached in one way or another from them; but so, too, were the fathers of fifty-four of the 100-man heterosexual group. And if none of the homosexuals had an affectionate father, only eight of the heterosexuals did. All the homosexuals had mothers who were loving or affectionate, but then, more than three-quarters of the heterosexuals did, too. Oddly, Dr. Bieber classified nineteen of the mothers of homosexual sons as either rejecting and hostile or detached, leaving one to wonder how, in the absence of close-binding mothers, those men ever managed to become homosexual.

It is hard to see how Dr. Bieber's supposedly typical parental characteristics are typical of anything or anyone. Of his 106 homosexuals, 27 per cent had been diagnosed as schizophrenic, 29 per cent as psychoneurotic, 42 per cent as suffering from a character disorder, and another 2 per cent as suffering from "other" disorders.* To serve as a valid control, his heterosexual group should, among other things, have contained an equal number of men suffering from the same mental illnesses. Dr. Bieber has never satisfactorily explained either how homosexual sons can be the end products of family constellations that do not fit his pattern or how heterosexual sons can be the end products of families that do.

Dr. Charles W. Socarides is another leading proponent of the doctrine that parents play an important part in causing homosexuality. In *The Overt Homosexual*, Dr. Socarides stated that the homosexual, not having been permitted to make the separation from his mother that normally occurs between the ages of eighteen and thirty-six months, retains an infantile closeness to her.

The male partners whom [homosexual men] pursue are representatives of their own self in relation to an active phallic mother. There are two parts to this concept. The first is an identification with a partner of the same sex. In this way they thereby achieve masculinity through identification with the partner's penis. The man chosen as a partner represents one's forfeited masculinity regained. The second part concerns the maternal breast: the penis of the male partner becomes the substitute for the mother's breast. . . . The reassuring presence of the penis in place of the breast allows the homosexual to feel that he is faithful and loyal to and simultaneously main-

* Bieber, p. 28.

85

taining the tie to the mother, but at a safe distance. . . . Furthermore, he is protecting the mother against the onslaught of other men's penises, allowing penetration into himself instead.*

This Rubegoldbergian approach to the human psyche was at one time held to make some sense, on the grounds, perhaps, of its being all but incomprehensible except to an elite. It is given little credence these days. Stripped to its essentials, it is merely a restatement of Dr. Bieber's thesis that close-binding mothers induce homosexuality in their sons—a thesis that, as we have seen, is convincing only to those who can overlook its myriad shortcomings.

Even the psychiatrists and psychoanalysts who continue to maintain that parents play a principal role in the etiology of homosexuality cannot all agree on the characteristics of homosexual-inducing parents. Dr. Lawrence Hatterer, a psychiatrist who specializes in the treatment of homosexual men, took almost a full page of his *Changing Homosexuality in the Male* to list fifteen maternal behavior patterns that various psychiatrists have associated with homosexuality in the son. A small sampling: "An absent mother, or the existence of too many overwhelming mother figures and/or surrogates." "An excessive dependency on the mother and her own dependency upon the son, with distorted mutual overidentification." "A mother's need or wish to be the sole authority and punitive disciplinarian in the family, resulting in the son's view of women as harsh, hostile, and to be feared or avoided."†

Dr. Hatterer's list of paternal behavior patterns that induce homosexuality is just as long. Again, to give only a few examples: "A father who turns to his son for affection

* Charles Socarides, *The Overt Homosexual* (New York: Grune & Stratton, 1968), pp. 63–64.
† Lawrence Hatterer, *Changing Homosexuality in the Male* (New York: McGraw-Hill, 1970), pp. 34–35.

(having been erotically rejected by his wife) and uses his son unconsciously for gratifications normally obtained from his wife." "A father who exhibits either one or a combination of the following patterns: absence, indifference, emasculation, aggressiveness, excessive dominance, hostility, rejection, partial and/or total inability to identify with the son." "A father who is homosocial—i.e., who dislikes the company of women but is only interested in them erotically, although his son is unaware of this."*

The reader will have noticed that many of these behavior patterns are contradictory. For example, an absent or an emasculated father is listed as being just as likely to cause homosexuality in his son as is an aggressive father or a father whose interest in women is only erotic; an absent mother is listed as being just as likely to cause homosexuality in her son as is an overwhelmingly loving mother.

The evidence that parents cause homosexuality is flimsy, to say the least. The most recent evidence implicates almost every conceivable kind of parent. Feelings of guilt on the part of parents are therefore misplaced, and should not be allowed to come between them and a homosexual son who, out of love and a desire to be open with them, confides in them. Mrs. Kameny's attitude strikes me as the best: "Accept them. Love them. *Show* them that you love them. And above all, don't blame yourselves."

* Hatterer, pp. 35–36.

CHAPTER SIX

# Homosexuals in Small Towns

In June 1974, after speaking to a gay group at Kent State University, I drove four miles east to Ravenna, Ohio— the last small town in which I had lived, the town in which both my parents had died. They had had many friends and I still knew many people there, but I did not get out to shake hands or say hello to anyone. I felt that by coming out publicly as a homosexual the year before, I had broken with the past. Now, driving down those streets—past the high school on whose playing fields I had failed crucial tests time and again in my father's eyes, past the house in which his hostility had deepened into silent hatred, past the church in which I had found so much warmth and no help—I experienced very little nostalgia. I did, however, regret that as an open homosexual I could never return to live and work in this or any other Midwestern town.

At Kent a young woman from Ravenna had told me that, so far as she knew, she was the only homosexual in town, and that she often had to drive as far as Akron for companionship.

The next day I spoke at nearby Youngstown State

University, where I got a possibly more authentic sense of Midwestern or Middle-American attitudes toward homosexuality than I had at liberal Kent State. At a press conference after my speech, a television reporter walked up, gazed at me for a moment as if he were wondering why I was wearing a business suit instead of a dress, and said: "As a queer or faggot, would you say that..." I stopped him in midsentence to ask if, when he interviewed blacks, he began by saying, "As a coon or nigger . . ." His surprised eyes revealed that he was experiencing the miracle of cognition.

Queer, faggot, fairy, fruit, coon, nigger, sheeny, Hebe, kike, wop, dago, spic, Mick, Chink, Jap, gook—I grew up with most of these words. Indeed, this red-blooded litany is associated with unenlightened small towns, with the heartland, with Middle America, although, of course, the bigotry that spawns these terms pervades the nation and every social stratum. Thus, when the homosexual flees his small, safe home town for the big, strange city, he cannot count on finding either a populace more enlightened or legal protection more humane than what he has left behind. He finds, if he is lucky, anonymity and others like himself— a subculture within whose purlieus and preserves he can find friends.

But what about the homosexuals who have stayed put in small towns? It is much too easy to say, "Let them move to the cities." Some cannot; others, rooted by temperament or background to the securities of rural life, have chosen not to. But whatever the reason the small-town homosexual remains in his community, he has a hard time of it. If he conceals his nature, he will remain unfulfilled; if he comes out, he will be looked upon as a freak.

Daniel grew up in a small town in the Midwest, the oldest—and the only adopted—child in a family of six.

After dinner the night he graduated from high school, his Baptist minister father announced that he had a present for him and handed him an envelope. Daniel sensed this was not to be a normal graduation gift—his brothers and sisters had been spirited out of the house, and his mother looked as if she were about to cry. He opened the envelope to find a one-way ticket to New York and twenty-five dollars. "Start packing," his father said. It was no use appealing to his mother; her only comment was, "I think this is best for the family."

Daniel went up to his room and packed. Into his suitcase he crammed a sports jacket, three shirts, and three pairs of pants, shorts, and socks. His father then drove him, in total silence, to the railroad station. His words of farewell were: "Good luck. I hope I never hear from you again."

It was two months after this that I met Daniel, a short, thin, long-haired eighteen-year-old who wandered into the offices of the National Gay Task Force. The nightmare of what happened to him before his father did what was "best for the family" and for the community sums up what all of us homosexuals who grew up in small towns feared would happen if anyone found out about us.

"My father," Daniel says, "is very intelligent and sensitive about a lot of things. He just has a closed mind about some things—sex, for one—because he feels that as a preacher, he has to set an example. He was a high school basketball star, and he's very popular with his congregation—very popular all over town, in fact." Daniel says his mother, a real-estate broker, is equally bright and well-liked in the community. It cannot have helped Daniel's self-image that his brothers and sisters were all tall and healthy. A small, frail child, he used to tag along after his mother. She kept his blond hair long until he was five and later encouraged him to help her when she cleaned

90

and cooked. Daniel's father compared this boy who was not interested in sports with his succession of muscular sons and found Daniel wanting, "a mistake."

When Daniel was fourteen, he had his first homosexual experience—"with an older boy in another town, when I was visiting my grandmother. I told my father about it, and he said that it was just a passing thing and I would outgrow it." A year later his parents walked into his bedroom and caught him engaging in oral-genital sex with another boy, the only other homosexual he knew in town, who was, in fact, more bisexual than homosexual. "The next morning, my father said, 'This is a sin. This is an abomination. Man was not made for man, nor woman for woman. You will go to hell.'" Daniel told me that his father repeated this warning almost daily for the next three years. When Daniel's parents offered to send him to a psychiatrist, he replied that he had read that psychiatrists could help only homosexuals who wanted to change their sexual preference, but that he enjoyed sex with boys and did not want to change.

In the fall of his senior year in high school, a girl developed a crush on Daniel. "She wanted me to go to bed with her. Finally I told her I was gay. She was the first outside person I had ever told, and I told her because I liked her and didn't want to hurt her.

"But she went and told her friends," Daniel continued, "and they told their friends, and the story spread like wildfire through the thousand kids till everybody knew that I was gay—the teachers, the guidance people."

That first day the students only stared at Daniel. Then, he said, "they thought they would have some fun and show what they thought of faggots. I would be walking down the hall and someone would kick the books out of my hands. One day there was a cherry bomb in my locker. The next day my books were stolen. I had to buy four sets of books that year. Then somebody stole a piece of my clarinet and twisted it in the shape of a penis, and put it back in my locker. I was knocked down the stairs at school twice. When I went into the lunchroom, I had to duck; one kid would throw an apple at me, another kid would throw a milk carton. And going back and forth to school on the bus, nobody would let me sit next to them, so I had to stand there listening to all the shit they were giving me."

The school authorities could not ignore the situation. They suggested to Daniel's parents that they give him the chance to start fresh at a boarding school. But for his parents this would have meant allowing Daniel—a hopeless sinner in his father's eyes—the right to live without retribution. The God-fearing Baptist minister refused even to consider it.

Realizing that they would have to act in Daniel's behalf where his parents clearly would not, the teachers and school board met in November and drew up an elaborate plan. Daniel was put in classes attended only by girls, allowed to go to study hall instead of gym and to eat his lunch in the teacher's room, and taken out of all extracurricular activities except the band. He was let out of each class three minutes before the bell rang, so that no one would have the chance to heckle or hurt him in the halls, and taken to the next class by the guidance counselor, who also drove him to and from school. Incredulous at these stories, I checked them out with the guidance counselor; they are true in every particular.

If the students could no longer pester Daniel at school, nothing prevented them from badgering him after school —or from telling their parents about him. "Kids from school worked in most places in town," Daniel told me. "If I went to a restaurant, I wouldn't be served. At McDonald's I ordered a hamburger, and the kid behind the counter threw it on the floor and stepped on it. I went into a supermarket and I heard three women talking about me: 'There's the preacher's kid who's a queer.' They went to the manager and he came up and said, 'I'm sorry, but you'll have to leave.' I couldn't go *anywhere*."

At home, too, there was no one to intercede between Daniel and his persecutors. Daniel's father set the tone with his continual warning that the boy would go to hell if he did not "stop being a homosexual." If Daniel tried to argue the point, asserting, for example, that "God is love, and if two men love each other God is there also," the harangue would turn into bitter argument. Sometimes Daniel's father would get so angry he would hit Daniel with the buckle end of a belt, and twice he shoved him down the stairs. Daniel's mother's attempts to reconcile the two were completely unsuccessful. Nor was she able to restrain her other sons: They called Daniel a faggot and kept their distance from him. "The only one who stuck up for me," Daniel said, "was my fourteen-year-old sister. But then my father would get angry with her. Once when he was knocking her around I told him to leave her the fuck alone—those were my very words. And I was so mad at him for hitting her that when he started down the stairs I pushed him, and he fell and dislocated his shoulder. I figured that made up for his pushing me down the stairs twice and whacking me with that belt."

The last four months of Daniel's life with father, family, and town were a concentrated hell as he became more and more literally a pariah. His father ordered him to take meals alone in his room so that he could not corrupt the morals of his loyal sister by spending any more time with her. And when several members of the congregation objected to his presence, Daniel was banned from his father's church—and its piano, which had been one of his few pleasures. Daniel went to another local Baptist church until students and their parents made it impossible for him there. He then tried a Methodist church, but was made equally unwelcome.

There was one ray of hope in Daniel's life: He was a virtuoso clarinetist and had won prizes in district, state, and national contests. In the spring of 1974, Daniel competed with forty other high school student musicians for a prize that included a scholarship to one of the best music schools in the country, which happened to be in New York. Daniel was one of the winners.

When Daniel arrived in New York early on a May morning in 1974, he was so exhausted that he took a room at the nearest hotel and collapsed. He had been too tired to ask how much the room cost. When he woke up that afternoon, he learned that his long nap had cost him the full twenty-five dollars his father had given him. Totally broke in a city in which he knew nobody, Daniel picked up his suitcase and walked thirty blocks south to a Greenwich Village gay bar, where he met a young man who invited him home. By the time Daniel found his way to the Greenwich Village office of the National Gay Task Force, in late June, he had lived with three men. Through the Task Force he found a job doing clerical work and has since moved into a small Village apartment of his own. He began music school last fall and keeps alive by holding down an assortment of part-time jobs. "I feel secure and happy in New York," Daniel says. "I can be openly gay here without anyone saying anything."

Daniel has heard from his mother a few times since he left home, and once she sent him a check for $200. But she cautioned him not to write back—she does not want her husband to know she is staying in touch.

Such rejection is cruel, but Daniel is too busy now to brood about it. It is not only his studies and jobs and friends and lovers that occupy him. There is also the challenge—exciting, to be sure, but one that should never have been necessary—of learning to direct his energy from defending himself against attack to maturing, developing tastes and opinions, experiencing life in a relaxed and open way. Daniel has a lot of catching up to do. For him, New York was the answer.

Matthew, a thirty-five-year-old farmer, lives just outside a small Midwestern town. His story is nowhere near as dramatic as Daniel's, but it is more typical and, in its own way, just as sad. Daniel told one person he was homosexual, and the result was that the whole town turned against him. Matthew, who has kept his sexual preference a secret, is looked up to as a natural leader in his community. President of the local chamber of commerce, he is also an elder of his church, an officer of many farm groups, and a counselor for youth groups.

In the fall of 1973, just a week after he read a wire-service story about my coming out publicly, Matthew wrote to me. I was, he said, the first person with whom he had ever had an opportunity to discuss his homosexuality. "It is a relief to know that there is one person in the world with whom I can talk about this subject with the assurance that I will still be regarded as a human being."

A similar sentiment was expressed by all my small-town correspondents, and it is not hard to figure out why. Most homosexuals feel an acute sense of isolation when they discover their sexual identity. This sense must, realistically and naturally, be intensified when the discovery is made in an environment where fulfillment is impossible and social acceptance of the unknown a thing not even to be hoped for.

Matthew gradually opened up to me in his letters, although he remained so terrified of being discovered that he rented a post office box in another town to receive my replies.

Matthew was born in 1939 and brought up on the farm he now runs. His parents were "hard-working, religious, sincere farmers." They did not fit the stereotype of parents of homosexuals; his father was not hostile, his mother was not smotheringly protective. "I had a good relationship with both my parents, and neither was particularly strong or weak or loved me or my sister more than the other. We had to work hard, but we were all close." During his high school years Matthew found that he was attracted by "strong, manly bodies," but he did not regard himself as a homosexual: "I thought of homosexuals as effeminate, weak-charactered, and aimless fellows, and I certainly was not one of those." In college, however, he was forced to admit "how deep-rooted my attraction for men was," and that "my sexual fantasies had always been of making love with another man." This belated realization surprised Matthew all the more because, as he wrote, "I was very square in every other respect. I didn't drink or smoke or use drugs, I dated girls, I attended church regularly, I was good at sports."

Matthew has never had sex with another man, although he "would welcome and encourage such relations." He has continued to date women, "always avoiding any physical involvement."

I asked if he had considered joining a gay organization in a nearby city as a way of meeting other homosexuals. "I do not want to be on their membership lists," he explained, "even though I understand they're coded. I'd be too nervous somebody would find out." Also, he thought it unlikely that such organizations would attract the "kind of person with very high standards" whom he hoped to meet—an erroneous assumption, I pointed out in my reply.

Had he, I asked, considered moving to a big city? For one thing, he couldn't; his father had died, and now he had to run the farm and support his mother. But he wouldn't move even if he could. "If my father hadn't died," he wrote, "I might have worked for an advanced degree in animal husbandry, but I would have continued to live in or near a rural area. I love my work on the farm, and I get quite a lot of satisfaction out of community service."

Furthermore, he has had almost no way of obtaining accurate information on the kinds of lives homosexuals lead in big cities. He is afraid to risk subscribing to homosexual magazines or ordering homosexual books, and he is a full day's drive from the nearest place where he might buy such literature. "I've read articles—generally derogatory—about homosexuality in a number of newspapers and magazines," he continued, "and I also occasionally am someplace where I can purchase *Gay Times* and *Gay Blade*. The gay fellows in the stories lead lives so different from mine. I know that the picture I receive from these accounts is distorted, but I have no other source. Meanwhile, I'm looking for someone to talk to whose life is like mine, but there isn't anyone."

"It's his own fault," some may think. "If he really wanted to find gratification, he could take a chance and move to the city." Certainly he could. All he would have to do is leave his mother without support, abandon the farm to which he has devoted himself his entire working life, line up a job in the city, untangle himself from his comfortable network of social obligations, and take himself off to a place where he is certain he will meet no one who speaks his language. As simple as that.

In the midst of our exchange of letters, Matthew found himself, as counselor for a youth group, face to face with a high school student going through a sexual identity crisis similar to the one he himself had experienced in college. This student, however, had not only yearned and fantasized; he had also engaged in a great deal of homosexual activity. Matthew had known Andrew and his family for years without ever suspecting that he was gay. He felt un-

97

qualified to counsel the young man—"I know so little about homosexuality," Matthew wrote me, "that I find myself wondering about the same questions he asks me"— and promptly suggested that Andrew talk with the local doctor or consult a psychiatrist. Andrew said he didn't want to. Matthew did his best. In Matthew's words,

His greatest problem now is guilt. I have tried to impress upon him that one can be gay and still contribute much to society. He finds it hard to believe that there are homosexuals like those you have written to me about—doctors, lawyers, professors—because in the city where he goes to college he sees only those whom many of us do not wish to be compared with.

The thing I'm most afraid of is that he will ask me sometime if I'm a homosexual. I'm not sure what I'd say, though I don't think I could lie to him.

Andrew did not ask. A few months after he told Matthew that he was gay, he got married. Recently he reported to Matthew that he was confident that everything would work out for him. Perhaps, like many other uninformed homosexuals, he had plunged into marriage to fight his homosexuality.

Matthew's encounter with Andrew—the first avowedly homosexual man he had ever met—led him to see himself in a new perspective. For one thing, he changed his mind about allowing me to use his story in this book. At the beginning of our correspondence, he had written: "I would like to change the public's image of us, and if my story will help, please go ahead and use it. I can assure you, though, that change will come very slowly to small towns like mine—probably not within my lifetime." But then he refused permission because, he wrote,

I am afraid that other young men in similar situations in rural America may read about me and decide that they can live as I have, and I do not recommend my way of life to anyone. I am a homosexual, quite happy and capable of contributing to my community, but I am doing it by nearly impossible means. I have avoided all sexual relations; and I don't believe that this is mentally, physically, or socially healthy for young men. I don't feel it would be wrong for a young man to have such relations, but he could hardly engage in them to any satisfying degree and still live easily in a small town as I do. He would live in constant fear of detection and blackmail, and, should he ever be detected, his world would fall apart. I don't contend that I have more will power or that I have been less tempted or that I have less sexual desire than other healthy young men, but circumstances and conditions have been such that I can, with difficulty, lead a life that might destroy others. I pay a high price for this. I have to keep my distance from everyone. In this respect at least, mine is an impossible life.

Two months later, Matthew reversed himself again and granted his permission. "My change of mind," he wrote, "came as a result of a talk I heard a few days ago. The speaker stressed the worthlessness of homosexuals, whom he bunched together with sex maniacs, criminals, and the like. I was perturbed and wished I could send him a copy of your book."

Matthew continues to write, invariably inviting me to come to his state and go fishing or hunting or skiing with him. Since I am not a rugged outdoorsman, I respond by inviting him to come to New York, where he could meet homosexuals as responsible and moral as himself. But neither of us has gotten around to dropping in on the other's world.

Roger, a doctor who lives in a small Northwestern town, also wrote to me after I came out publicly. As our correspondence developed, we, too, invited each other to cross the country for a visit. Roger accepted; in the winter of 1974, at the age of fifty-one, he came to New York and met other homosexuals socially for the first time in his life.

Before coming east, Roger had opened up his life to me in a series of letters. (Again, I was the first person to whom he had been able to mention his homosexuality.) Roger was born and brought up in a small Wyoming town, where his father was a professional man. His first memory of any sexual feeling, he wrote, "goes back to when I was five or six. I was lying on the living room floor, on my stomach, looking at a *Tarzan and the Apes* comic book and imagining how it would feel to be over-powered and held in Tarzan's arms."

Roger was eight when his father died. "Those were difficult years," he recalls. "My mother moved often, and my older brother and I kept having to change schools." Then his mother remarried, and there were new problems. Roger remembers his stepfather with little affection. "There was something rough and brutal about him, about the way he spoke, moved, reacted." The boys' mother be-gan to drink heavily. "When I came home from school," Roger recalls, "I never knew whether I would find her sober or drunk on the kitchen floor, with her husband storming out of the house."

Roger had his first homosexual experience when he was a sophomore in high school. "There was a dark, muscular boy who sat across the aisle from me. One day the two of us walked along the railroad tracks that led out of town. First we walked arm in arm, then arm on waist, then each of us reached down for the other. We stumbled down off the embankment and tumbled together in the grass and opened each other's flies and hugged and masturbated each other. Later, neither of us spoke about what we had done."

Throughout his high school years, Roger dated girls. In his senior year, he went steady with a girl, whose company he enjoyed "so long as I wasn't left alone with her." Roger preferred the company of an older boy he knew, a "handsome guy I'd go for long drives with almost every night, but nothing ever happened between us."

After high school, Roger enlisted in the Navy, as did his brother, who, Roger says, "I now believe was a homosexual, too. But he was killed in action in the South Pacific before we could talk about it." It was during his four-year stint in the Navy that Roger accepted his sexual identity. "Again and again I formed friendships with men, but I never dared to be openly sexual with them. In my last year in the Navy, a buddy and I brought two women home, and while he was fucking his woman on one bed I tried like mad to fuck mine on another bed. But my buddy's body interested me more than the one underneath me."

After the war, Roger attended a college in Baltimore. He spent twelve years there—finishing college, going to medical school, doing his specialty training. His medical education completed, he drove west "and came upon this beautiful town way up in the mountains that just happened to be in need of a doctor. I settled in, and it's been my home ever since."

How could a thirty-five-year-old, well-educated homosexual put himself in such a position? Didn't he realize that by choosing to live in a small town he was choosing a life that would afford no chance of love? Had he learned nothing about gay relationships during his twelve years in Baltimore? Roger's decision to settle in a small town was as baffling to me as, at the time, it must have seemed natural to him.

Roger explained that throughout those twelve years on the East Coast he had been too busy to lead any sort of social life: "The money from the GI bill wasn't enough, so most of the time I had to hold down a series of part-time jobs that kept me busy from 6:00 P.M. till 1:30 A.M. I was a grind in every respect—not by choice, by neces-

101

sity." And even when there was time, he had been too frightened to make sexual approaches to men: "I fell in love with a handsome medical student. We shared an apartment for a few months, but we never became lovers. Then he moved into a fraternity house, where he roomed with another friend of mine. For the last two years of medical school I had to endure the sight of the two of them sitting side by side in the lecture hall every day." Roger wrote me that during his stay in the city he never —knowingly—met a single homosexual and never heard of the existence of a gay bar—"though I now realize that in a city of that size, there must have been at least half a dozen of them." Roger hoped someone would pick him up on the street; no one did. He looked for information about homosexuality—unsuccessfully. "I am well aware, now," he wrote me, "that books on the subject existed even then, but I scoured the card catalogues of four libraries and came up with nothing." Thus, when he drove west, Roger was "medically well educated, but an ignoramus concerning almost everything relating to my sexual identity."

Roger's quick decision to settle in a place that necessarily precluded his having a regular sex life is a good example of the doublethink that plagued homosexual men of his and my generation. We may have had countless homosexual experiences—certainly we had countless homosexual desires—and we may have managed to go on leading productive, even creative lives. But on some very basic level, we were unable to reconcile these two things and accept ourselves as worthwhile individuals who happened to prefer sleeping with men to sleeping with women. Roger blurred the issue and denied his sexual nature— which meant, in effect, denying himself any sex life. When his timid efforts to find gay companionship in Baltimore had failed, how much easier it was to abandon the issue and ensconce himself in an environment where it would seldom

102

come up—particularly when that environment seemed perfect to him in every other way.

As a new bachelor in a small town, Roger was quickly invited to a series of supper parties, at which he was introduced to a series of unmarried women. In his nearly seventeen years of living in the town, Roger wrote, he formed one close friendship with a woman, and it ended badly. "She was a widow, attractive and charming; we had many intellectual and cultural interests in common. We became inseparable—socially, that is. But as the years passed and I failed to show any physical interest in her, she became increasingly upset. I, for my part, could not even fantasize a physical relationship with her, as I found it difficult even to touch her with any tenderness. A relationship that had once been pleasurable soon became intolerable for both of us. I took to staying at home, listening to music I loved, reading books, walking my dogs. Of course, I also had several men friends to go hunting or skiing or fishing or hiking with."

Roger's first adult homosexual experience occurred on a hunting trip when he was thirty-nine. He and a friend had spent the day out hunting together. "The cabin was very cold. Soon after supper we bundled together under layers of blankets to go to sleep. I woke up and found that Jack was stretched out alongside me. He was a trucker, with powerful shoulders and chest muscles and strong legs. I turned to him with my hand across his stomach. I let it stay there, and he let it stay there. Then he put his hand on my stomach. I stroked his chest and he just lay there, hardly breathing, saying nothing. Then I moved my hand down and he opened his legs and let his knee drape over my thigh and then he moved his knee up toward my groin. Then his hand touched my penis, and we caressed and massaged each other until orgasm. He didn't say a word, and eventually we fell asleep.

"The next morning we woke back to back. Neither of

us spoke about what had happened. Early that morning we shot a beautiful bull elk high on a ridge, and we spent the entire day lugging the quartered elk down to the road. We've never gone hunting together since. The following summer he got married. He has a child now. For about a year, whenever we passed on the street, he gave me this odd look."

Roger's only other adult sexual experience occurred in Vienna, where he was on vacation. "I went to a steam bath. The attendant informed me that this was a bath for homosexuals. I said, 'Well, that's fine.' I took a room, and soon a young man entered, with a hopeful look on his face. I gathered that he did not speak English, so I motioned him to lie down beside me. It was very good—much better than anything I'd ever dreamed about. Afterward, we lay for a long time gently stroking each other, and then he left. I felt I had to see him again, to find out his name, where he lived, and I rushed down the hall after him. I asked him his name and where he came from, first in one language, then in another and another. He explained in gestures that he was a deaf-mute."

"It is curious to think that you, a stranger, now know more about me than anyone else in the world," Roger wrote me when we had been corresponding for a while— "a fact that pretty well sums up the isolation of my life. The thing I miss most is not being able to be *close* with someone else. There are other, smaller tribulations. It is considered good sport in these parts to joke about queers and fairies. Even the doctors I meet crack jokes about queers. And I laugh right along with them, of course.

"I'm not saying there are no pleasures in my life. I love my practice and this town and these mountains. I have allowed myself to be absorbed into this landscape which, seventeen years ago, made me decide, in my wisdom and ignorance, that this was the place for me."

Roger stepped out of his landscape for a week in the winter of 1974 to come to New York. He was looking forward, he wrote, "to learning how to open myself up to new relationships."

He looked like a Westerner—tall and rangy, wearing a conservative suit, a deerskin vest ("I shot the buck and I made this myself"), and a string tie. At first he was reserved, almost diffident. He spoke with a slight drawl, and he walked with the long stride of a man not accustomed to stopping for traffic lights. I introduced him to gay activists —priests, professors, schoolteachers, men who were half his age and who dressed casually. He did not feel altogether comfortable with them. "I'm so used to hiding, and they're so open, and the politics of homosexuality is all new to me." I introduced him to my older physician friends, with whom he felt more at ease: Perhaps the common bond of medicine helped him adjust to the novel situation of finding himself in a roomful of other homosexuals. Another shock for Roger came when I took him to the swearing-in ceremony of a new commissioner of health, an old friend of mine. A large number of city officials made a point of greeting me and coming over to talk. It was not, I explained to Roger, that I had been a particularly popular administrator; rather, these people were going out of their way to show that my coming out publicly three months before had made no difference in their attitude toward me. He could not understand it; general support for a public declaration of homosexuality would have been unthinkable in his home town.

Perhaps I should never have shown Roger that there was a world in which a known homosexual could be accepted and respected. But it was my world and I wanted to share it with him. I did not stop to think that it might be cruel to flaunt my personal freedom in the face of a man who had grown accustomed to living in emotional confinement.

I suppose I even felt it was possible that Roger would decide to give up the comforts of his small-town life and settle in New York.

At a party given by a gay physician friend of mine, Roger met a young man with whom he spent the rest of his time in New York. Before he returned home he told me that they had arranged to meet for a Western vacation sometime in the summer. As for New York City, he didn't like it. He didn't like the dirt, the air, the noise, the bustle. He couldn't wait to get back to his quiet house, his dogs, his practice, the mountains—and even to the townspeople, with whom he shared an aversion to big-city life.

A month later he wrote me, quoting a passage from a New York *Times* book review: " 'Like everything which is not the result of fleeting emotion but of time and will, any marriage, happy or unhappy, is infinitely more interesting and significant than any romance, however passionate.' " This sentence, he said, epitomized his thoughts and reflections during the flight home. He had since arrived at the conclusion that "transient affairs with strangers in cities will, like romances, never be satisfying. It is only under stable conditions that, through the workings of time and will, romances can lead to the establishment of anything permanent and begin to assume significance. I wish I had understood this twenty-five years ago! It would seem to follow, then, that I shall never know a significant relationship—at least so long as I live here. So my alternatives are to remain here and give up the hope of ever living with someone I love, or to leave. And I suppose that I have already made my decision by living here for so many years. For whenever I return to this small town, I feel as if I am coming home, even though it's to an empty house."

This letter both heartened and saddened me. Roger was clearly the wiser for his New York trip, but at the core of the wisdom he had gained was the certainty that there were things—vital things—that he would never have.

Life is, of course, choice, and each choice precludes a host of other possibilities. Roger has made his bed, so to speak, and now must lie in it. Those who disapprove of us homosexuals and feel that we should abstain from all sexual activity rather than indulge our "sinful" desires will no doubt applaud his decision. My young gay activist friends, on the other hand, would see Roger as a man who, swallowing the code of the straight world whole, has rendered himself useless—to himself and to the other homosexuals for whose cause he might have fought. I do not feel that either of these extreme positions is fair.

No one who has not had the experience of discovering he is homosexual in a tightly knit community, where traditional values are the only values and moral issues sort themselves tidily into black and white, can quite grasp how difficult it is. Mere survival is hard; survival with a semblance of self-esteem is harder, since one has grown up with the same values that now condemn one. And standing up to be counted—alone—to face seemingly universal opprobrium is more than can be expected of most people. I know I would never have had the courage to do it if I had settled in Ravenna—or in almost any other small town in America. Small-town life imposes conformity; I am certain I would have succumbed and spent my whole life trying to pass as straight.

Homosexuals have won a certain degree of acceptance in the large cities. But the final victory for homosexual freedom will have to be won in the small towns. It is easy enough to grant acceptance to a group of people one sees oneself as never having to associate closely with. It calls for a greater degree of understanding, for a true change of mind, to welcome such a group of people into the intimate society of a small town.

107

CHAPTER SEVEN

# Married Homosexuals

Before I came out publicly, I knew very few gay men who were married. Married homosexuals travel in different circles; their straight domestic and social lives leave them no time for a gay social life as well. Few have lovers within the gay community. When they cannot resist their homosexual urges, they are much more likely to pick up men in Turkish baths, public lavatories, and other such places.

After I came out, many married men wrote me, telephoned me, or came to visit me. Married physicians who had read about me in a medical magazine came from as far away as California to talk, so great was their sense of isolation and their need to air their problems. A number of gay married graduate students whom I had met at New York University sought me out. And a lot of the gay activist leaders I met were married—though still more of them were divorced. The high incidence of married or formerly married men in the activist movement must be a sign of a special desire on their part to publicize the truth about homosexuality. So many of them had been deluded into believing they were straight—and marrying to prove it—

because they saw no resemblance between themselves and the garish stereotypes of gay men that were paraded as scientific fact.

Technically, of course, almost all married homosexuals are bisexual, in that they can perform sexually with members of both sexes. According to Kinsey, 37 per cent of adult American males have had at least one homosexual experience to the point of orgasm.* Most such men, Kinsey found, engaged in homosexual acts when they were physically or sexually isolated, from either women in general or their wives in particular—in military service, in prisons, in logging camps, and so on. A recent study† of men who use public lavatories for homosexual encounters found that 54 per cent of the men were married, and that 8 per cent were separated or divorced; that 44 per cent of the still-married men were Catholics, and that their wives (also Catholic) resisted having sexual relations. For these men, homosexual encounters were a substitute form of sex that had a major advantage over heterosexual affairs: They were free of emotional ties. All of these married men defined themselves as heterosexual.

It is not this group I am going to discuss here, but rather those men who feel they need male love and prefer sex with men to sex with women.

The married and formerly married homosexuals I will describe are all physicians, Ph.D.'s in some scientific field, or doctoral candidates in the health sciences. All, then, should have known far more about homosexuality than the general public does. And yet nothing in their backgrounds had prepared them to recognize their sexual natures. If

* Kinsey *et al.*, *Sexual Behavior in the Human Male*, p. 637.
† R. A. Laud Humphreys, *Tearoom Trade: Impersonal Sex in Public Places* (Chicago: Aldine Publishing Co., 1970); and "New Styles in Homosexual Manliness," in *The Homosexual Dialectic*, Joseph A. McCaffrey, ed. (New Jersey: Prentice-Hall, Inc., 1972).

these men could stumble into marriage, one can only wonder how many thousands more go to bed every night with
wives whose bodies cannot give them as much pleasure as a
man's, and how many women sleep next to men whose
coolness to them wounds and confuses them.

Dr. T.—a middle-aged Japanese-American orthopedist—
called me from the airport one evening in December 1974
to ask, in a confusingly indirect way, if I were the Dr.
Brown who had come out publicly as a homosexual. When
I told him I was, he said that he had flown in from the
West Coast, chiefly to speak to me. He was so nervous that
I was reluctant to let him come to my house; he sounded
more like a junkie than a physician. But as he had flown so
far and his distress was so obvious, I told him I would see
him.

Dr. T. was one of the most frightened men I have ever
met. As I opened the door, he stammered an apology for
being so indirect over the telephone—he had been afraid
the operator might be listening. His whole body literally
shook with fear. Only after an hour and more than one glass
of bourbon did he calm down enough to talk coherently.
For weeks he had looked forward to meeting a fellow gay
physician, he explained: he had never been able to speak
to anyone freely about his problem. He was forty-nine,
and he felt as alone in the world as I had as a medical
student.

Dr. T. told me that he had had homosexual experiences
during his adolescence, but that they had left him feeling
so guilty that he had stopped. Passing over the subject in
his mind, he had been too fearful to ask himself what
those experiences must have meant. Then, in medical
school, he had met a woman medical student whom he
liked a great deal. They had similar views on a number of
things (including premarital sex—as devout Catholics,
neither of them approved of it), and Dr. T., leaping at

110

this chance to blot out his past misgivings, married her. He had hoped—prayed, even—that his homosexual urges would leave him once he married. They didn't; instead, his desire for men grew. "For four or five years I kept thinking I would get over it," he told me, "and when it would not leave me I began to feel hopeless. I loved my wife; we had a child. If I gave in to my urges, I knew I would destroy my family life and ruin my professional life. Many mornings I would go to church and pray for help. Eventually I gave that up, and then I gave up believing in God altogether. If there were a God, why wouldn't he help me? My problem was so real and so great."

Dr. T. subsequently consulted two psychiatrists, but for only one session each. "The first was so expensive that I never returned, and the second told me I didn't need therapy. I was much too tense and frightened to express how strong my feelings were. Both of them told me the same thing: that I couldn't be a homosexual because I hadn't had any homosexual experience for years. I did not argue with them because I realized that if I did convince them, word about me could get out."

Dr. T. was forty-two and the father of three children when he had his first adult homosexual experience. "The desire became uncontrollable. I went to a gay bar and I went home with a man. That night left me feeling just as guilty as when I was a boy, and much more frightened— now I was a husband and a father." Since then he had had a number of one-night experiences, each one adding to his burden of guilt and fear. He hated himself for giving in; he despaired at finding the encounters almost not worth the pain—they were strictly carnal, offering him none of the spiritual companionship he craved. At permanent war with himself, Dr. T. had come to believe there was no way out—not even a truce.

As he spoke, I sensed that part of his problem stemmed

111

from his own nature: There was a brittleness to him that would have made adjusting to any complicated situation a challenge, and a tendency toward self-denial that led led him to reject, categorically, the various solutions or compromises I tried to suggest. No, he could not contemplate separation or divorce—he loved his wife and children. No, he could not even speak to his wife about the conflict that was tearing him apart—she would never understand, it would only make things worse. But how fully society had cooperated with his nature in building the walls of his cage! Homosexuality had been so horrifying to Dr. T. that he hid from accepting it in himself until it was too late.

But knowing that one is homosexual early in life is not necessarily the answer. As a young man, Jim was well aware that he was gay—in fact, he began having homosexual experiences when he was sixteen. At twenty, he sought help from his family physician. It was not that sleeping with men made him feel guilty; rather, he wanted to have what his middle-class upbringing had taught him every man should have—a wife and family. "I felt I wouldn't be complete otherwise," Jim explained to me. "I still feel that way."

Jim's physician referred him to a psychiatrist who specialized in treating homosexuals and who outlined a very definite program for him. Jim was to give up homosexual experiences, to avoid the company of gay people, and to continue therapy, at least until he felt ready for a lasting heterosexual relationship—in short, the same prescription my analyst had given me twenty years before.

Jim had been in therapy for four years when he met a young teacher, also in analysis. He dated her, enjoyed her company; they made love (Jim had had only one brief affair with a girl, in high school); and, six months later, they got married. Like Dr. T., Jim had latched onto a woman whose unwitting function was to prove he was straight.

In some ways, Jim's attitude toward his marriage is a calculating one: He is reasonably pleased, since it is providing him with the things he expected of it, and he manages to preserve superficial accord by avoiding all mention of his homosexuality, past or present. He wants to have children—"I have a very strong paternal instinct"—and intends to remain married at least long enough to do so, possibly longer. Meanwhile, the only overt problem in the relationship is sex. Jim is not as happy with sleeping with his wife as someone who was pronounced "cured" by a psychiatrist might hope to be; in turn, although he is able to perform with her sexually, he finds he is not comfortable touching and caressing her—it does not feel right to him—and he is always aware of disappointing her. To ease the situation (from his own point of view), Jim has had numerous brief affairs—always with men. Although these have been of the clandestine pickup variety, they have given him a measure of sexual gratification that his marriage has not.

Ostensibly, as I said, Jim is somewhat calculating; he has tried very hard to work out answers to all the questions about his situation that anyone, including himself, might ask. But I had the feeling as we spoke that he was skating on the surface of a panic that might very well engulf him. Guilty about his duplicity as well as his inability to please her sexually, Jim has repeatedly suggested that his wife have extramarital affairs. She has been understandably upset about this, assuming that it means he is seeing (or at least contemplating seeing) other women. Jim is both afraid to be honest and afraid to lie; he has persistently replied only that a lot of other women find him attractive. His wife's retort to this—that a lot of other men seem to do so as well—is an indication that the delicate fabric of half-truths supporting their relationship may be wearing thin.

The effort of juggling so many games at the same time has left Jim with no very clear idea of who and what he is. He refuses to consider himself gay but finds the label "bisexual" equally objectionable and inappropriate. ("That's the word for upper-class people who go out and have a homosexual experience once or twice and then go back home to the wife and kids and feel, 'Well, now I've tried everything.' ")

At least in one area of his life, Jim may soon have to face the facts. More and more he is teasing his wife into guessing his sexual nature: "I have a thousand masks," he told me, "and my wife is getting inside more of them than anyone else ever did." It is cruel to maneuver her into doing his psychic work for him—peeling away the layers one by one until he is forced to confront himself—but for Jim, too, there is a lot of pain in store. What will he do when his wife, aware at last that he is homosexual, and incensed at all the years of deception, leaves him—as she almost certainly will? With his crutch gone, Jim will have either to commit himself to being what he is or to wander indefinitely in a limbo-like state.

Dr. Claude W. was thirty and had been actively homosexual for nine years when he married. It was 1960, and he had had three years of analysis. I had met Claude in 1955. There was a strange but typical dichotomy in his life, in that his private practice was predominantly straight, but his social life was almost entirely gay. Claude had been living with a young man for five years when I met him, though not monogamously. In fact, he and I were occasional lovers, and once we spent a vacation together in Europe. While I primly visited museums and galleries,

Claude, provided with a list of gay places, set off in pursuit of sexual adventures.

It was during this vacation that Claude told me how much he wanted to be heterosexual and that he had been seeing an analyst for three years in the hope of changing his sexual preference. Women were not unknown to him; he had dated girls in high school and had had sexual relations with two or three young women in college. Heterosexual relationships were more meaningful than gay relationships, Claude felt; and he wanted very much to be a father.

A few months after we returned from Europe, Claude told me that he had shared a beach cottage with a group of young single men and women and that he was beginning to have heterosexual dreams; his analyst assured him that soon he would be having heterosexual relations again. Not long afterward, Claude fell in love with an Armenian woman whom he married within the year. Since almost all Claude's friends in New York were gay and he wanted to make a fresh start, he moved with his wife to another city.

Claude has been married for fourteen years now and has three children, of whom he is immensely fond and proud. Each time we meet, he tells me that he greatly prefers his heterosexual life to his former gay life but that he still considers himself a homosexual. Why? "I enjoy sex with my wife," Claude told me, "but most of my dreams and all of my fantasies are gay. And I still have homosexual urges that are just too strong to deny. About once a month I have to make love with a man."

I asked Claude what role analysis had played in his life. He replied that it had, perhaps, helped him to relax with women and hence to feel more comfortable making love to them; but that in no real way had it changed his sexual feelings. I asked him if sex with his wife were as pleasurable or satisfying as sex with a man. "No," he said.

The married homosexual men I have met have difficulty imagining how deeply their conflicts are hurting their wives. I believe it is guilt that causes this: Realizing that their wives are as capable of suffering as they are themselves—and as aware of being unfulfilled—would make the burden too heavy to bear. Joan, a graduate student whose former husband, Patrick, discovered he was homosexual while they were married, was eloquent in describing what those years were like for her.

Joan and Patrick really loved each other—deeply and on a number of levels—but this only made their three-year-long marriage even more agonizingly complicated than it might otherwise have been. Both bright, both sensitive, both struggling for self-awareness, they spent those years alternately embracing and lacerating each other; tranquillity entered their relationship only after they were divorced.

They met in 1964, when Patrick was a graduate student and Joan was still working toward her bachelor's degree, and slept together for the first time that winter. Joan had never had sex with anyone before; Patrick had had extensive experience with women—had even gone so far as to become engaged twice—but he had also had a homosexual experience that he was at pains to explain. He told her about it, admitted that he was attracted to men, but didn't seem to feel it meant very much. Certainly it didn't mean he was homosexual—that word, Joan recalls, was not even mentioned. "I was too young and naïve to know anything about it, and too closed to ask anybody who might have known. If it happened now, of course, I would wonder what the hell I was getting into. Anyway, we *both* got into it."

At the same time he was preparing to move in with Joan, Patrick found himself attracted to a man. Then, before he could bring himself to ask Joan to marry him, he went through an elaborate routine of asking her what her answer would be if he *should* decide to propose. Joan's answer was "yes" to both questions, but then she got cold feet when her parents failed to raise the anticipated objections—"It is much easier to argue than just to know you are doing the right thing." Their wedding night was prophetic: They had known each other sexually for months, but that night they were constrained and awkward.

"Marriage was something that we blundered into partly out of love, partly out of insecurity, and partly out of habit. It was a rude awakening in a way, because you think you know someone and all of a sudden you're married and you don't know them." As soon as they got back from their honeymoon, Joan remembers, Patrick began to pull away. He found excuses to spend many more evenings in the laboratory than before, and she was perhaps not too surprised when he brought home Larry, a fellow graduate student to whom, it turned out, he was attracted.

Patrick was still too confused, too inhibited, and much too insecure in general to ask Larry to go to bed with him. Instead, the three of them carried out a farcical compromise. Larry came to dinner at least once a week; Larry went to movies with them; Larry was an ever-present family friend. But as soon as Larry had gone home, Patrick would confess to Joan how much he wanted him, how much he hoped Larry could be the friend *and* lover he knew he needed, how fearful he was of being discovered as well as rejected if Larry turned out not to be gay.

Because he needed so desperately to share his confusion with someone, Patrick kept Joan informed of every step in his journey toward coming out. She got to know about all the crushes he had on the men he worked with; she heard of his experiences, at first timorous, then more bold, at the

117

athletic club steam room; she learned about his sexual experiences with men, his constant and fruitless searching for a man who could give him what he wanted—"He was looking for a friend and he was looking for a lover, and there were times when he settled for a lover. But he really wanted the whole thing with a man." She ruefully remembers one particular incident, when she came home and somehow just sensed that Patrick had had a lover there while she was out. "I remember saying, 'How could you bring anyone home? There weren't any sheets on the bed!' Because"—a sad, self-mocking laugh—"I was out doing the laundry. I mean, it wasn't so important that he had gone to bed with someone in our house, but that the house wasn't presentable!"

Even as he was becoming more and more overtly homosexual, Patrick tried to avoid pinning that label on himself. "We had been married about a year when he said he thought that if his marriage were everything it should be and everything he wanted it to be, he wouldn't want men. There was something wrong with our marriage, and so he wanted men. For a long time I believed that."

At this point, Joan went to the university's mental health clinic in search of some help for herself. Patrick didn't mind, although he himself refused to go—one brush with counseling in his undergraduate days at Harvard had convinced him that talking about his feelings with an outsider was too painful to consider. After a couple of sessions, Joan told the therapists that her husband thought he was a homosexual. "They thought they'd hit on the problem right there; they thought they'd got it." The psychiatrist they assigned her to "sat there like he had all the answers, but he wasn't going to tell me because I had to figure them out all by myself."

Which was terribly difficult to do. It might have been simpler if things had been all bad, but even now Joan feels

118

—and believes that Patrick would agree—that their marriage had been better than most. "There was feeling and love between us. We did things together almost constantly. We had a lot of the same interests. It *wasn't* boredom. There was always a lot of humanness between us. On the other hand, there were times when there was a lot of pain on both sides—there were scenes. I almost always knew when he had been with someone, even when he didn't tell me. Patrick cared for me—that was perfectly obvious—but it was *tearing* to have him say that he also cared for someone else." Tearing enough that she began to talk about divorce. The mere word upset them both. Fearing perhaps that by leaving him she might be throwing him irrevocably into homosexuality (or into utter solitude, which was worse), Joan dropped the subject.

They had been living like this for about two years when Joan met a man she was attracted to and who—salve for her battered ego—was attracted to her. "I was in a pretty vulnerable state at that point. This was the first man who had really paid me a great deal of attention and complimented me since I had been married. I was fairly indiscreet in showing that I liked him. A relationship developed, and eventually it turned into an affair."

Irrationally but understandably, Patrick couldn't help being fiercely jealous. "Which I thought was hysterical. The whole thing was hysterical, but it wasn't very funny." Now there was another twist, another sore issue to be batted back and forth between them in their endless effort to define their relationship and themselves. Patrick, striving to maintain dignity as well as the marriage, finally announced that he would understand and accept her having affairs—but this particular man wasn't the right one for her. Joan remembered how upset he had been at her confession, however, and decided not to make a second: Although she had a few affairs in the last year of their marriage, she said nothing at all about them to Patrick.

Joan's finding gratification with other men took some of the pressure off the marriage and allowed it to continue, but their equilibrium was tenuous at best. The most obvious area of deterioration was their sex life. Joan—bruised, ambivalent, and half-numbed after so many onslaughts of emotion—found she had very little passion left for Patrick. And *his* attention was focused on whether he was making love to his wife with sufficient frequency to qualify as a masculine man. "Two times a week . . . well, that wasn't enough. Was three times a week okay? Or four times?" Nevertheless, perhaps sensing that an actual rupture in their sexual relationship would make it impossible not to rethink their marriage, Joan and Patrick continued to go through the motions.

Until the spring of 1968, when Joan was unhappy enough to give Patrick an ultimatum: "The men or me. 'I love you,' he said, 'and it's you, and I'll give up the men.' Six weeks later he came back to me and said, 'I can't do it.' So it was dumped back in my lap. And at that point I wasn't strong enough to say, 'Well, if that's the way it is, then we've had it and let's split.' "

Joan wonders if she would ever have found that strength if Patrick hadn't met Gordon, who promised to be that combination of friend and lover he had been hoping to find. "I knew that this was someone he really cared for, and so I just decided we should split. From that point on, my life was much more hopeful. It was also absolutely devastating, but it was more hopeful."

Patrick moved out gradually, spending a few days with Joan and then a few with Gordon, and the time before he left was one of high emotion for all three of them. "Patrick and I weren't sleeping together, and it got so that I didn't want to stay in the same bed with him. I was angry and hurt. I didn't want him physically, but I didn't know what I wanted. I did, and I didn't, want to be alone." Patrick was also torn. He wanted very much to help Joan, to show her how much he still loved her; but Gordon was jealous and resented any time he spent with her. Even Gordon's position was ambiguous. By unhappy coincidence, he had been a childhood friend of Joan's, had known and liked her up through their high school days; taking her husband away from her was a source of sorrow and regret to him.

Indecision continued in Patrick's life long after he moved in with Gordon. Joan remembers that just before their divorce went through, he was still having qualms, still wondering if it might not be best to try to repair the damage and stay together. They have gone on seeing each other, although Gordon tried to forbid it. Recently Patrick said to her that in some ways he feels their marriage was much better than his relationship with Gordon is. Even though he has been exclusively homosexual since they broke up—he still lives with Gordon, in fact—Patrick does not yet feel that he is permanently, totally gay. He speaks from time to time about eventually sleeping with women again . . .

There is no bitterness now in Joan's feelings about Patrick. She is realistic about how much her own insecurity and ignorance contributed to their predicament ("That was the price I was paying for not being smart enough to say, 'Why do I have to put up with this shit?' "); she is grateful for the ways in which he helped her grow as a human being; and she is aware that it was his own real anguish that made him hurt her. Because they were so close, she got a very vivid sense of what it was like for him to discover he was homosexual and to try to balance his various needs and desires— his search for a complete relationship with another man, and his desperate wish just to be with a group of people in which he was not in some subtle way out of things, which ultimately outweighed his attachment to her. But more than anything else, she is left with a paradoxical question: How is it possible to have known someone so well and yet have never understood something as basic about him as his sexuality? "It's a whole different world. We could be walking down the street...I would be looking at the men, and *he* would be looking at the men. His gayness was something I understood and I didn't understand. It was like trying to look at the world through another person's eyes, with another person's brain. You can't really comprehend how different it all looks."

Joan and Patrick were perhaps fortunate in having been so young and, except to each other, unattached when his discovery came. Children, and the rituals of family life involved in raising them, can make the process of uprooting himself and starting over long and agonizing for a homosexual man.

Christopher is a scientist who did not really accept his homosexuality until he was thirty-six; by then, he had been married for eight years and had two children. His wife divorced him two years later to marry another man.

Christopher grew up in a small town in Maine; like Patrick, he had had homosexual urges well before he married. In 1952, when he was nineteen, he talked to his minister about his attraction to men and asked if this meant he was going to be a homosexual. The minister's reply, Christopher recalls, was, "A fine young man like you? Nonsense." Christopher explains: "He was reacting to stereotypes just like I was. I was tall and strong and a good athlete—I'd won a lot of ski meets and I was a quarterback on the football team—and I came from a good family, so I couldn't possibly be queer. Meanwhile, I looked at the one man in town who everybody said was queer—a very effeminate type—and I was pretty sure I wasn't whatever he was. So I was more than ready to believe the minister."

Two years later, when he was a junior in an Ivy League college, Christopher was still worried about his gay fantasies and yearnings. He consulted a psychiatrist, who asked him if he had had any homosexual experiences (Christopher had not), questioned him about his family life (Christopher enjoyed a warm, close relationship with both parents), asked him about his interests and aims, and concluded that he was simply passing through an age of sexual anxiety and was definitely heterosexual. "He backed his argument up," Christopher said, "by saying that homosexuals weren't built like me and that they weren't interested in sports—or, if they were, they weren't good at them. He was the second man to insist that there was no need for me to worry, and since I didn't want to believe I was queer in the first place, I allowed myself to be convinced. And I stayed convinced for years."

When he was twenty-eight, Christopher met and married a twenty-four-year-old medical student. "I loved her—I still do—and we shared a lot of interests, and . . . well, marriage was the thing one did at a certain age, and I was that age." Christopher had had no sexual experience with either men or women before he married; his wife had lived with a man for six months when she was twenty-three.

Christopher never enjoyed sex with his wife, though he was able to satisfy her. After being married for about two years, he found "I could achieve orgasm more easily if I fantasized that I was having sex with a man." He tried not to think too much about that, though.

For the next two years, all seemed well on the surface. It was an extremely productive time professionally—Christopher finished a book, published a number of scientific articles, and received a generous foundation grant to pursue further research—and, ostensibly, a happy time domestically. "My wife was getting her specialty training as a surgeon, and I took care of the children many evenings," Christopher told me. "I felt a real love and sense of responsibility for them. And Ellen and I certainly enjoyed each other, helped each other, entertained, did lots of things with the children. We quarreled occasionally, but our fights were no more frequent or bitter than anyone else's."

Christopher simply could not identify himself with the stereotypical homosexual. Besides, he had no idea what homosexual life was like, having never met an avowed homosexual (though it turned out that a number of his colleagues were also gay). And—perhaps the strongest reason for not coming out—he was worried that any attempt to venture into the gay world would jeopardize his marriage. "It was more than two years after my first vague realization that I *must* be gay that I did anything about it," Christopher told me. "At first all I did was go to the stores on Forty-second Street that sell magazines with gorgeous men on the covers. I leafed through them, bought a few, and threw them away before going home. Finally, after several months of this, I managed to ask the owner of one of those stores where such men hung out. He pointed to a bar down the street that had a big 'This is a raided premises' sign on the door. It took me another couple of months to work up the nerve to go in. I sat in that bar all night—a thirty-six-year-old man nervously waiting for somebody to pick him up and introduce him to real life. Of course, no one did."

But two weeks later Christopher had sex with a man he met in another bar, and from him and from subsequent sexual partners he learned where to find men in and around New York City—at other gay bars, at the gay section of a city beach, at a number of Turkish baths. "These 'relationships,' " Christopher said, voicing a common complaint of homosexuals who have not yet established a community of friends, "were more impersonal than I wanted them to be. At the baths, for instance, I could meet a man and hold him in my arms for two or three hours, but that was it. And anyway, it was hard to invent excuses to stay away that long, so I could only get down to the baths about every two or three weeks. I could never have a warm relationship. I was terrified when someone asked my name or where I lived or what I did—not the best attitude for relaxing and getting to know people."

Preoccupied as he was with this problematic new element in his life, Christopher failed to notice that his wife was becoming increasingly remote. It was a shock to him when in the summer of that year, she announced that she was going off by herself to France for a month to think, leaving Christopher in charge of the children. "She didn't even leave an address; we had no way to reach her," Christopher said.

Shortly after she returned, Christopher suggested that they visit a psychiatrist for marriage counseling. It was now obvious to both of them that they needed help. During their sessions with the psychiatrist, whom they saw singly and as a couple for nearly a year, they experienced a number of revelations. Halfway through the year, Christopher's wife announced that she was in love with another man and wanted a divorce so that she could marry him. Almost simultaneously, Christopher guardedly admitted to the psychiatrist that he was homosexual; the psychiatrist suggested that he tell his wife.

Neither of them was able to greet the other's news with understanding. Christopher was outraged. It did not occur to him that his wife, after several years of living with someone who always half-wished he were with someone else, might have been compelled to find comfort and love with another man. Not yet ready to commit himself to life as a homosexual, and sensing that a divorce would leave him no rational alternative, he clung to a raft of platitudes for safety: She had been unfaithful and that was terrible, but he loved her and the children and did not want a divorce. Christopher's wife's reaction to *his* announcement was even more indicative of how little they knew each other: She simply refused to believe it. "When I told her I thought I was a homosexual, she said she knew I wasn't, and if I thought I was, it was probably just a reaction to her plan to divorce me. I would get over it, she said."

Several months later, over Christopher's objections, they were granted a divorce. His wife remarried. Christopher, frantic and rudderless at first, plunged into a series of brief homosexual affairs; finally, he got to know and love a colleague, with whom he still lives.

I asked him if he could describe the difference between having sexual relations with a woman he loved and with a man he loved. "I enjoyed touching my wife," he said, "but I felt no profound desire for her, as I did and do with men. I was much less interested in prolonged foreplay than a basically heterosexual man would be. When you're lying there wishing you were with someone of the same sex— because a man's body is such an exciting and beautiful thing—you hold back. The rich emotional charge is missing. I didn't get those deep feelings from my heterosexual life, none of that extraordinary sense of support and the simultaneous need to be supported, even though I loved my wife and still do. The fulfillment that comes from being the person I should have been all along is a great thing for me."

Christopher has come to believe that he should have told his wife about his homosexuality much earlier than he did, and that all gay husbands should tell their wives as soon as they discover who they are. "It's important for the wife to have that knowledge," Christopher said, "so that she can make up her mind about what she wants to do. We've all been duped by society into thinking marriage is the only way to live. The husband and wife should probably divorce so that each can go on to a more fulfilling life, though they must try to work out an amicable way of caring for their children."

Christopher's wife has custody of their children, but she has granted him full visitation rights. He sees them frequently, takes them camping in summer and skiing in winter. He wanted them to get to know his lover, but his wife threatened to have his visiting privileges restricted unless he saw the children alone. He has, however, told his children that he is a homosexual. "I felt I just had to be honest with them," Christopher explained. To have sidestepped the issue—while their continued relationship with him made it clear that there was an issue being sidestepped —would have destroyed their trust in him. Far better, Christopher felt, that his children confront the possibly disturbing fact of his homosexuality than that they grow up in an atmosphere of mystery and suspicion, with his absence unexplained and the reasons for it festering in their minds. Furthermore, "if they turned out to be gay— though I don't think they will—I wanted to be able to help them; I did *not* want them to waste thirty years of their lives discovering who they were and possibly even getting themselves into contractual agreements they would later regret. And even if they didn't need this help, I wanted them to be tolerant of people who do, because I think that kind of open-mindedness spreads to other areas, too. All my kids have been able to deal with the situation, but I *am* concerned about problems they'll face in their early teens. Kids in that age group are exquisitely sensitive to peer comment and ridicule. So far my kids have not been teased, but then they're lucky enough to live in a rather sophisticated community."

Christopher's decision to be truthful with his children is backed up by almost all experts on child rearing. They agree that in such cases, the children should be frankly talked to, in terms suitable to their age and maturity, about the father's sexual orientation and the nature of his relationship with his lover, and that acquaintance with a parent's homosexual "spouse" is not likely to upset or harm a mentally healthy child. The important factor, most authorities say, is that the child see that the parent has a warm relationship with another person—of whichever sex. There is also a general agreement among the experts that a person's sexual orientation does not make him or her any less capable as a parent and that there is no evidence that homosexual parents are more apt to raise homosexual children. Thus the suitability of a parent to have custodial or visitation rights must be judged independently of his sexual nature. As Dr. Benjamin Spock wrote: "[These questions] should be decided on such bases as the parent's devotion to his child, his sensibleness in managing the child, evidence of his child's love of him, his general ethical standards." Dr. Judd Marmor, President of the American Psychiatric Association and professor of psychiatry at the University of California, Los Angeles, has said: "I know of no evidence that predominantly heterosexual parents are more loving, supportive, or stable in their parental roles than homosexual parents."

It is astonishing that neither Christopher nor his wife—he a biologist, she a physician—was able to acknowledge his sexual identity for all those years. The resultant suffering is inestimable. Christopher had become a family man; he was attached to his wife and to his children by bonds of love that were painful to break. But he blames neither himself nor his wife for being so slow to recognize the fact. "Society," he says, "defined what a 'queer' was in a way that made it obvious to me—and others—that I couldn't be one. Then it kept telling me that if I was one,

I was a lost soul anyway, an outcast—which meant that I consistently tried to ignore the evidence. Against odds like that, even a trained scientist has a hard time establishing the facts."

The men I have described here should probably never have married, but it is easy to understand how they stumbled into it. If society says that homosexuals are, by definition, effeminate, weak-minded, narcissistic, superficial, and worthless, is it not natural that a person would strive—desperately—to prove that he is not one? It is the rare and fortunate homosexual who, discovering his gay impulses, is not struck with fear and horror of them; one's own body, it seems, condemns one to membership in some sordid underworld where all human values and decent satisfactions mean nothing. Some men are able to combat the stereotype and establish comfortable lives for themselves within a gay community; others struggle to compromise with it—because their homosexual urges are too strong to resist, or because they are discovered and forced to commit themselves before they are ready. But some, finding a woman for whom they feel genuine affection at a time when they have not yet resolved their sexual confusion, are lured into fighting one myth by embracing another: that marriage makes men, that having and supporting a family is the ultimate proof of masculinity.

And once married, the homosexual man finds himself in chains of love and association that are hard to shake off. He is human, after all; living with his wife over a period of years, albeit in frustration, he becomes attached to her and does not want to hurt her. And mixed with the guilt over contemplating leaving her is the guilt over never having been all she needed either. Besides, he may have children; emotionally and financially he is bound to them.

Beyond this, there is the effect of simple habit. Think of the heterosexual couples you know who have lingered in unhappy marriages, inventing countless excuses to stay together, because they were afraid that however unsatisfying their day-to-day routine was, being alone might be worse. For a homosexual, this fear is compounded. Throughout his marriage he has probably seen only the worst side of the world he is thinking about entering— the baths and bars and public lavatories—and, lacking contact with a settled homosexual community, has no way of believing that he could be any happier outside the security of his family than within its confines.

Bruce Voeller, whom many still-married homosexuals have sought out for advice since he came out publicly in 1971, believes that most of them remain married. "They feel a lingering love or obligation to their wives, and they don't want to hurt them or hurt their children. Also, a number of years into marriage, they feel that they're too old to attract a man and that it's too late to start a new life. They feel that they are trapped and will never know real closeness and warmth with another person. Many hope that their wives will stop wanting to have sex with them. Most of them have had very few homosexual experiences; some, because of religious or moral convictions, have never had any. In one way or another, they all say the same thing: 'It's as if we had locked ourselves into a prison.' "

# CHAPTER EIGHT

# Long-Term
# Relationships

Marriage is not the only way a homosexual man can have a long-term relationship. A number of us have enjoyed stable, lasting relationships with other men, relationships that offer us all the opportunities to grow with and through another person that marriage offers heterosexuals. But by and large we are a group that the public—including many homosexuals—knows nothing about.

There are certain reasons for our obscurity. Tending to be more comfortable with his life than an unattached homosexual, a man involved in a long-term gay relationship is less likely to show up in the psychiatrist's office— and hence less likely to show up in textbooks. As he is also much less likely to be found "cruising," the law has not encountered him, and heterosexuals who have based their opinion of gays on the flagrantly effeminate types they see on street corners are not even aware of his existence.

But he exists, and it is my hope that as society's attitude relaxes and increasing numbers of homosexuals feel free to regard themselves as complete human beings, there will be more and more like him.

I am not arguing that a long-term homosexual relationship is problem-free—no intimate contact between people ever can be—or that establishing, nurturing, and maintaining one is a smooth, easy process. In fact, we have some snags and pitfalls to cope with that many heterosexual couples do not. But such relationships are the only rewarding alternative for those of us who do not want to live in either the closet or the bars; and, as my own story will show, they are possible.

One major issue, however, needs to be discussed at the outset: promiscuity. This is the most frequent and notorious criticism of our long-term relationships, by the people who know we have them—a criticism often pointed to as proof positive that we are incapable of serious attachment. Such wholesale condemnation is a facile bit of "do-as-I-say" reasoning coming from heterosexuals: Is every married man who has an affair considered an emotional invalid?

Nevertheless, it is true that promiscuity is more common in the homosexual world. Among the established couples I know, about a third are completely monogamous, a third allow each other total sexual freedom, and a third (behaving a good deal like the proverbial errant spouse) have occasional affairs, which they try to conceal from their partners. I am not speaking here of homosexuals living completely promiscuously, though of course there are such people, nor of homosexuals who regularly engage in partner-swapping, group sex, and other activities indicative of an obsession with sex. That kind of behavior seems futile to me—whether it occurs among homosexuals or heterosexuals—because its rewards are so limited. Even that third who allow their partners total sexual freedom feel primarily bound to the men they live with; for many of them, this seeming dichotomy presents no problem.

There are some logical reasons for the incidence of greater promiscuity among homosexuals. Most of us were obliged, at least in the beginning of our gay lives, to find sexual gratification in a series of one-night stands; promiscuity was an ingrained and, however grudgingly, accepted part of our tradition. And even when we are able to find long-term partners, we know that our sex life is illicit. We are therefore crossing no clear barrier when we step out of our legally unauthorized unions to engage in "extramarital" affairs. Besides, if monogamy has served the historical function of keeping the family together, and the primary reason for not breaking up the family is to protect children, we who have no children are without that compelling reason to be strictly faithful. Nor are we deterred from being promiscuous by the deeply rooted belief that sex is properly a part of marriage and is justified by having children. A further curb to married men does not apply to us—the fear of making our partner-in-sin pregnant and becoming entangled in new unwanted responsibilities.

But these reasons are all excuses to explain away an unpalatable fact. The gay activists who banded together after the 1969 Stonewall riots had begun to clear the air take a different view of the situation. They have been questioning the validity of many straight practices that homosexuals have used as models. Is monogamy essential to a long-term relationship? Does it contribute anything vital? Most of these young activists feel the answer in both cases is no.

I am not sure how I feel about it. Certainly promiscuity has drawbacks; but then so does a rigidly enforced—and unwilling—monogamy. Perhaps the most one can say is that each person, heterosexual or homosexual, must decide for himself, in accordance with his own needs and not in violation of others'.

I am almost hesitant to offer the story of the most important relationship in my own life—not because I am ashamed of it, but because it is hardly a model for others to follow. There were mistakes on both sides; we have not lived happily ever after. And yet Thomas enriched my life immeasurably; our love for each other has outlasted the differences between us; and perhaps our very imperfections will help demonstrate that it is possible for homosexuals to plunge into deep human relationships, with all the entanglements and inconsistencies those relationships entail.

I had lived with Steve (the muscular young man who turned out to be so surprisingly inhibited) for almost a year, then with a man ten years older than I for almost three. Steve's successor and I enjoyed entertaining a wide circle of friends, but this turned out to be all we had in common. Ultimately, our life together was hollow. He was an educator whose range of interests extended not much beyond the playground of a big-city private school or the back yard of a brownstone. Soon we were less lovers than co-hosts who happened to share an apartment. During the summer of our last year together, I went off to Europe. When I returned, I realized that we had drifted even further apart. Soon afterward we split up. I did not miss him so much as I missed having someone to have meals with and talk to, even over the gulf of our disparate interests, at the end of a day. Which is just to say that I was lonely.

For a few months I returned to the promiscuous life I had lived before meeting Steve. Then, in the fall, I met Thomas—in my own living room. One of my guests had called to ask if he could bring along a doctor friend who had come up from Richmond for the weekend.

On first impression, Thomas seemed arrogant to me. But after the others left he stayed on to talk, and I discovered that his arrogance was, as arrogance often is, only a shield for shyness; he had felt ill at ease, he said, among so many strangers.

Thomas had grown up on a California ranch and had been close to both his parents. Having helped his father with the chores, he was something of a jack-of-all-trades—a capable carpenter, plumber, and electrician. His mother had taught him how to cook and to can. I was surprised to hear him talk openly about his kitchen skills. He had none of the fear of appearing effeminate that even then made me pretend not to be interested in cooking. Tall, strong, and altogether able, he took his masculinity for granted.

We found that we had much in common. Thomas, too, had discovered his homosexuality in college; he, too, had had his first homosexual experience while attending medical school; he, too, had gone through an initial period of denial. He had never thought of seeing a psychiatrist, though. For one thing, he doubted the validity of the psychiatric claim that homosexuality was an illness. For another, his discovery that he was a homosexual had not deeply troubled him, and he had quickly entered into a number of months-long affairs. Doing his specialty training in a relatively small town had restricted his sex life for a few years, but in Richmond, where he moved to take a research position, he had been having many fairly brief affairs. Until me, he had never been involved in a long-term relationship.

The fact that we were both doctors was not as central to our relationship as might have been expected. Thomas was a laboratory scientist; I was primarily interested in putting medical services at the disposal of a wider public. Again, Thomas was a conservative—in health matters as well as politics—while I was very much a liberal. What bound us together, apart from our sexual compatibility, was that we were both ready to settle down to a domestic sort of life and found each other the right ones to share it with. Thomas was a good cook; I was a beginner, and he took pleasure in teaching me. We both liked to read and to talk about the books that interested us. And we enjoyed driving—through the Virginia hunting country when I spent a weekend with him, and through the New England countryside when he came up from Richmond to be with me.

Precisely when the two of us realized that we had become a couple I no longer recall. One warm spring day, when we were lying side by side in the sun in the back yard of Thomas's suburban house, I said I wished we could share more of our lives than just weekends. Thomas matter-of-factly replied that he would start looking for a suitable job in New York as soon as he completed the project he was working on.

I returned to New York wanting to tell the whole world my news. After all these years of searching for and finding and then realizing that I had failed to find a man with whom I could fully share my life, I was certain that I had at last succeeded.

In the months before Thomas moved to New York, I told all my gay friends about him and gradually introduced him to them. When my mother came to New York, I introduced him to her—as just a friend, of course. I took Thomas to dinner at my sister and brother-in-law's in Westchester. It was an uncomfortable evening. Everyone tried so hard to be nice. Jule and John wanted to make Thomas feel part of the family. Jule served a marvelous dinner; to ease the tension, John kept our cocktail glasses filled. The problem was that neither of them felt free to refer even indirectly to the nature of our relationship or to acknowledge the occasion—as formal an announcement of our union as I knew how to make. The conversation was mainly about gardening. In spite of his ease with other homosexuals, Thomas had never been able to tell a straight person that he was gay, and he found it hard to accept that Jule and John must know. The problems of the evening were, perhaps, insoluble, since none of us could do anything to make the others feel more comfortable. I know Jule would have helped if she had known how; when I had my heart attack, she quickly grasped that from my point of view, if not the hospital's, Thomas was my next of kin and should be allowed to see me in the intensive care unit and, later, to look after me at home. Over the years Thomas has grown more relaxed about her knowing that he is homosexual, largely because she has accepted our relationship in such a natural and, at the same time, thoughtful manner.

Perhaps we were trying to prove something. In spite of the awkwardness of that evening with Jule and John—who knew we were gay—we resolutely plunged right back into the family scene. Thomas asked me to dine with his parents when they were in New York. Both Thomas and I felt compelled to choose our words with such care that when the evening was over we collapsed, as exhausted as if we had been doing a balancing act on a very high wire for hours. From then on, Thomas visited his parents alone in the country, and I visited my relatives alone. Our social life as a couple, we decided, had better be exclusively gay—a rule we have generally kept to ever since.

Thomas moved to New York, and we took a large two-bedroom apartment—the two bedrooms for appearance's sake, since I knew that I would occasionally be entertaining straight friends. Our apartment was in a cooperative building, whose board of directors, like most such boards, required character and bank references. Thomas and I could not risk purchasing the apartment jointly. I bought it; the deed was in my name only. Officially, Thomas was just a guest.

I had lived with other men before, but fixing up this

apartment with Thomas was a very special experience. Each minor decision was invested with great importance, even joy—where the bookshelves should go, what shade of paint was best for every corner of the place. We did most of the work ourselves—enthusiastically. We were not just making a comfortable living space; we were building the home that we would share.

Since we both enjoyed cooking, we usually dined in. I cleaned the house between the maid's twice-weekly visits. We could have afforded a full-time housekeeper, but that would have presented problems. We could not have talked freely, nor would our guests have felt at ease. Then there would have been the daily routine of making it appear that Thomas and I did not sleep together—mussing the unused guest-room bed and putting used towels in the guest bathroom, and so on. We were not being paranoid; neither of us envisioned being "turned in" or lectured by a disapproving housekeeper. Having a potentially hostile person constantly in our home—or going through elaborate measures to prevent her from suspecting—was quite enough of a deterrent.

At first we were monogamous, unconsciously modeling our relationship on a heterosexual marriage. We did not exchange vows or go through any sort of ceremony, as some homosexuals do, yet we took it for granted that, having found each other, we would be faithful. Then I learned through a "friend" that Thomas had been sleeping with another man. I was hurt and furious; Thomas was abashed and remorseful. Later—much later, as I'll discuss more fully in Chapter Nine—I learned that it was my work that was starting to drive a wedge between us. But at the time Thomas could not explain his action at all. We picked up the pieces of our relationship and lived together in fragile harmony for six more months. Then I learned he was sleeping with someone else; once again, I exploded and he repented. The next step was, I suppose, predictable: I had an affair, and Thomas found out and got angry. I was less penitent than he had been, though—after all, I told myself, he had set the pattern. For some months the two of us took turns playing aggrieved lover and repentant sinner until, at last, it dawned on us that we were not really all that disturbed by each other's occasional affairs. What mattered most was that we still loved and believed in each other. This realization made us much more comfortable. Perhaps we could not (or did not want to) offer each other complete sexual fidelity; that lack, if a lack it was, in no way reduced the significance of everything else we shared. In time, Thomas and I stopped living together. But we have never stopped caring for each other, and I am confident we never will.

One basic problem in homosexual long-term relationships was touched on in my situation with Thomas, though we were lucky—for us it was an inconvenience, not a tragedy. I am speaking now of secrecy—the need to conceal from almost everyone the nature (and consequently the importance) of the relationship, and the emotional and practical ramifications of this. It did not enhance our feeling of permanence and stability that Thomas was technically a guest in his own home, that we could not see each other's families or entertain colleagues without travestying our feelings for each other. Grateful for the home life I was able to create with Thomas, I am reluctant to examine too closely how things might have been without all those precautions we had to take. But it is impossible not to be affected by one's own actions. Even if those actions are undertaken solely to deceive outsiders, no human being is sufficiently compartmentalized to resist the implications of his own behavior. By bowing to the constant, needling reminder that no matter how happy and natural they feel, theirs is a socially unacceptable union, homosexuals themselves undermine what could be the most rewarding aspect of their lives.

The consequences are more obvious and can be far more devastating in the practical sphere. Our society has a vast body of law to protect the property rights of persons who are divorced or widowed. A homosexual who is separating from his long-term partner must rely on that partner's good will to get his share of their jointly owned property (and I do not believe that good will is a very common element in the property negotiations of divorcing heterosexual couples!). And a bereaved homosexual stands a good chance of losing everything, at a time in his life when he is least capable of fighting. Unless the deceased lover had a carefully drawn will, his surviving partner has no rights whatsoever.

I know of a homosexual couple who had lived together for twenty-one years. One of the men died suddenly of pneumonia. A week after the funeral, his brothers appeared at the apartment; they had come to pack up and move out his furniture, paintings, tableware—everything. The two lovers had bought many of these things together over the years, but the apartment belonged to the deceased. The surviving partner told me that he believed that his lover's brothers had long suspected that theirs was a homosexual relationship and that now the brothers were, in effect, challenging him to defend his right to any of the belongings. He said nothing, and was left with nothing.

Forewarned, of course, homosexual couples can prevent this sort of thing (though I have known of cases where the family of the deceased contested his will, where, once again, the homosexual is caught in a vicious circle, for the law does not allow him to marry his partner, but at the same time it cannot assure him that his partner will inherit his estate because the two men were not married). What is almost impossible to avoid, until and unless society recognizes homosexual relationships, is the shock, the horror, and the utter loneliness of facing a bereavement without any of the traditional consolations. Relegated to the status of mere friend, the surviving partner must watch helplessly as members of his lover's family move in and establish their claim as next of kin, as they make funeral arrangements their own way, possibly shipping the body out of town. The fanfare surrounding death in our society is a tried and true way of protecting mourners from the first few weeks of grief, distracting them and at the same time acknowledging the importance of what they are going through. Not only must a homosexual face his grief without such support; he is also obliged, unless he is in an unusual situation, to completely hide what he is feeling. This sets up an unbearable emotional cul-de-sac. I have known men to be shattered by it.

A homosexual trying to make his way in a long-term relationship is like a member of any minority group making an incursion on territory hitherto forbidden: He must be stronger, braver, and wiser than everyone else to avoid foundering. If we were omniscient, we could arm ourselves against every conceivable mishap before it occurred. Failing that, we can only hope that society will grant us more and more legitimacy and, in the meantime, try not to swallow the prevailing image of ourselves. The deeper our conviction that we are valuable human beings who can love and be loved, and the greater the dignity with which we face our problems, the harder it is going to be for anyone to force us into hiding and shame. And long-term relationships are, among other things, one of the best proving grounds we have: What, after all, demands as much strength, courage, and wisdom as learning to live happily with another person?

# CHAPTER NINE

# Work

It was my homosexuality that determined my choice of profession—I hoped to solve the riddle of my sexual identity in medical school. It was my homosexuality that determined which city I would live and work in—New York would allow me to lead the sort of life, social and private, that my staunchly gay nature impelled me to. And it was my homosexuality that lay at the root of my decision to resign some eighteen months after I had attained the pinnacle of my profession. At the same time, my professional life repeatedly impinged upon my life as a homosexual, ultimately damaging the relationship that meant more to me than any other—indeed, more to me than anything else in the world: my long-term love affair with Thomas.

In the spring of 1974 I flew out to Minneapolis and emotionally relived an episode that can serve to bring into focus some aspects of the connection between the homosexual's life and his work. I had been invited on this trip as a known homosexual doctor to address a gay activist conference. In 1956 I had gone there as a supposedly straight doctor to be interviewed for a job I wanted very much.

I was then working with the Health Insurance Plan of Greater New York. I had hoped to find a position in one of HIP's group practice units, which provide medical assistance to those insured by the plan. This would allow me to be a practicing physician, which was my goal. (I could not establish a private practice when I came to New York because I was broke and deeply in debt to my Detroit psychoanalyst, and because I knew next to nobody.) Although the position HIP offered me was administrative, it had its compensations, and I took it. The job—my title was director of professional services—not only provided me with an entrée into the New York medical world, but also left me free to spend my nights and weekends as I chose. Moreover, I sympathized with the aim of the HIP program: to provide high-quality care for a fixed annual sum. This program of the fifties subsequently served as the model for both President Kennedy's and President Nixon's plans for restructuring the national health system.

In the Minneapolis job I would be heading a program, one which I also found inherently attractive: a cooperative prepaid group-practice health-care program that would be, in effect, owned by the patients. The doctors would work for them, full time, and would be responsible to them.

I had learned this much through an exchange of letters and telephone calls with George Jacobsen, president of a cooperative insurance company in St. Louis, who proposed to set up the Minneapolis program. No thirty-two-year-old physician interested in medical care reform could have asked for a better job. I flew out to Minneapolis full of hope but, as a man who had fled the Midwest not long before, with some misgivings.

Jacobsen picked me up at the airport and drove me

through beautiful pine woods to the small clinic that was to be enlarged as the program grew. I liked what I saw.

Later, at a cookout at Jacobsen's home just outside Minneapolis, I met other people active in the cooperative movement. I was impressed by them and also by the political support they had been able to muster (both the Lieutenant Governor and the Attorney General were there).

That evening, Jacobsen formally offered me the job. Delighted and grateful and proud, I nevertheless asked him to let me have a day or two to think it over.

As soon as I was alone, I did what most gay men do when they are visiting a city in which they know nobody. I went to a gay bar. This time, however, I did not go only to find a partner for the night—Steve and I had recently broken up and I had yet to meet the boyish headmaster with whom I was to co-host parties for those three increasingly cheerless years—but also to find out about gay life in this Midwestern city. The bar was dark and practically deserted. A customer informed me that it was the only gay bar in town. I spent the night with this man. When, on our way to his apartment, he asked my name, I instinctively invented one—something I had not felt compelled to do for some time in New York. I could see I would have to be very careful here.

The next morning on the plane back to New York, I realized that I could not accept the job. What if I were to be seen entering the one gay dive? Even if I were lucky enough to find a lover and establish a circle of gay friends, how could I live? I would be working for a group of very friendly people, the men and women on the board of the cooperative, and Midwestern folkways are pretty informal. In New York it is customary to call before you drop in on someone. But in Minneapolis? The thought of Mr. and Mrs. Jacobsen coming by while I was giving a gay party or merely sitting at home with a lover was chilling. If they, or some other straight couple, did not realize I was gay the first time they popped in, they surely would the second. No, I would have to remain in the East and stick with the job I had. (Ironically, Minneapolis has shown more tolerance and understanding of homosexuals than has New York City, as I learned on my return trip last year. In 1974 Minneapolis passed a gay civil rights bill closely resembling the one the New York City Council rejected that same year. Moreover, surveys taken before the bill was voted on showed that 70 per cent of the people in Minneapolis favored antidiscrimination legislation for homosexuals.)

But if in this instance my homosexuality interfered with my career, it also helped by keeping me in New York. Professionally, my problem was how to keep my medical skills intact while parking for a time in an administrative slot. Ways opened—to the grand detour that ultimately led to my becoming health services administrator.

Shortly after my arrival in New York, I was appointed to the faculty of the Columbia University Medical School as a part-time instructor and also to the staff of Bellevue, a rundown city hospital affiliated, however, with a medical school that had an excellent teaching service program.

In 1956, I volunteered my services to Beth Israel Hospital, where I spent one night a week seeing patients in the cardiac clinic. Both here and at the Bellevue clinic I plunged into my work with such fervor that I gained the reputation of being a particularly conscientious clinic physician. And indeed, I cared very much about my patients, and tried to treat them with the same consideration as my great-uncle had treated his in Hebron, Ohio.

Most clinic patients are poor. The well-off go to private physicians and are not accustomed to being kept waiting long; sometimes their doctors even make house calls. I felt a special empathy for the poor. My Cleveland and Detroit ghetto experiences had served to jar me into an awareness of how much they suffered at the hands of a medical establishment that tended to regard them as a human subspecies fit to be used as guinea pigs. But I think that my long battle with homosexuality was a factor as well. I, too, knew what it was like to struggle with a problem and go on struggling and still get nowhere, to feel permanently beaten, and, worst of all, finally to be convinced that one deserved nothing better. The humiliation I often saw in my patients' eyes was something I had learned to conceal behind a doctor's professional calm. Under that mask, even then, in the mid-fifties, I believed that being homosexual meant that I was psychologically impaired—a born loser, like the poor.

In any event, my work in the Beth Israel cardiac clinic impressed the hospital's director, Dr. Mark Freedman, so that when in 1961 Beth Israel, a voluntary hospital under contract with the city's Department of Hospitals, took over Gouverneur Hospital on the Lower East Side, he proposed that I be put in charge. And I enthusiastically accepted.

I have already described my work at Gouverneur; here I shall touch on only those aspects of it that relate to my homosexuality. Obviously and foremost, had I not been a homosexual I would have remained in the Midwest and been a small-town family doctor like my uncle. That had always been my dream. At Gouverneur I felt compelled to reconcile this dream with the big-city slum background, to bring small-town warmth and personal care and involvement to the impersonal metropolitan scene. My homosexuality had driven me into exile, but I hoped at least to re-create a portion of the atmosphere it had forced me to relinquish.

What a mess I had walked into! All hospital services had been closed down and patients rerouted to Beth Israel. Mice scurried through the clinic offices; the walls and ceilings were falling down. Patients had to wait for hours

146

in gloomy rooms—only to be prodded into cubicles where physicians, many of them all too glaringly incompetent, proceeded to treat them without respect. I set about chasing the mice out of the building, if not the incompetent doctors. They simply could not grasp the new doctrine that called for a drastic change in dealing with patients: From now on each patient would be given an appointment—which was unheard of in clinics—his own physician, and an opportunity to complain about his treatment.

Looking back, I suppose I hired a few more homosexual physicians than a straight doctor would have. Those who knew about my homosexuality and about the changes I was making at Gouverneur referred their friends to me. I certainly did not seek out homosexuals, and they always remained a distinct minority on my staff. Some of them ranked among the best, also demonstrating the genuine concern for the poor that was essential to my concept of how Gouverneur should be run. Others of these young homosexual doctors on my staff, like many men and women in medicine, lacked this concern; courteous in dealing with their patients, they did not give that extra measure of warmth and understanding that the old, for example, especially need. In both attitude and performance, then, the gay minority was indistinguishable from the straight majority.

There were times when the presence of gay doctors on my staff made a real and constructive difference. For example, gonorrhea, which is often spread through homosexual contact, was assuming epidemic proportions in the neighborhood, but for some weeks no young men came in to be treated for it. By chance, the first teen-ager to show up was seen by a gay doctor who succeeded in bringing home to him the need for prompt treatment; the boy spread the word, and shortly thereafter kids turned up in droves.

My homosexuality was indirectly responsible for another aspect of my hiring policy. Everyone who works in a hospital in New York is required by law to be fingerprinted. Most hospitals, eager to keep out anyone with a police record, rigidly enforce this rule. One day a young man who had applied for a position at Gouverneur told me, at the end of our interview, that he could not risk being fingerprinted since he had once been arrested on a charge of accosting and soliciting another man "for lewd purposes." He insisted that he had been innocent and that he was not homosexual, adding, as if to prove the point, that he was married. (He didn't know that I was homosexual, and I didn't tell him.) He seemed right for the job. I told him I would arrange matters so that he would not have to be fingerprinted, and I hired him.

Having broken this rule once, I continued to break it whenever it seemed wise to do so. I hired a young black man just out of a Southern prison; I hired a number of people from the neighborhood who had police records. These men and women made particularly good staff members. They understood what I meant when I said that the poor were to be treated kindly and with respect. If at the same time I treated these former criminals with more respect than they were used to, I did so mindful of the fact that I, too, had committed illegal acts. The only difference was that I hadn't been caught.

Between bouts of firing and hiring, I was busy tearing down and rebuilding. The old building had to be repaired and brightened. Thomas kidded me that my real interest in Gouverneur lay in the fact that it gave me a chance to play the interior decorator. Actually, I was afraid of revealing my homosexuality by showing the slightest interest in color schemes and the like. I stuck so relentlessly to such manly jobs as tearing down walls and carting junk out to the street that in the end Mark Freedman had to bring in a color consultant to transform a clinic that had looked like an anteroom to the lower depths into a cheerful place.

All in all, the new Gouverneur was a great success. The number of patients using the clinic more than quadrupled —from about 45,000 in 1961 to some 200,000 in 1963—as word got around of the prompt attention and considerate treatment we were dispensing. The health community, too, began to take notice of what my colleagues and I were doing, and I rose notch by notch, becoming consultant to the Office of Economic Opportunity in Washington, D.C., and then Mayor Lindsay's health services administrator.

Those years were the best of my life. Thomas had moved up to New York to live with me, and we were very happy. My professional life was tremendously rewarding. As best I could, I had bent the dream I had brought from the Midwest to the grim realities of life on the Lower East Side. My staff and I had brought a touch of Ohio to a community that was sorely in need of a sense of community. We visited settlement houses and churches and schools to talk about our program. The volunteers we had attracted greeted, welcomed, and served refreshments to patients confined to the clinic. I often wish that I had never left the work I began and the people I came to know on the Lower East Side.

As I rose in my profession, the distance between Thomas and me grew. My work with the OEO, for example, often required me to be away from New York for days at a time. Thomas had to do all the household chores that we otherwise shared. And while he did not mind sharing them, he did not enjoy starring in the role of housewife. Also, as I became more involved with health care programs for the poor, I got to know a number of gay doctors and health professionals. Whenever I invited a group of them home to dinner, the conversation inevitably turned into shop talk, and Thomas would feel left out. If my doctor friends brought their lovers, Thomas would be stuck with the chore of making small talk with them. He was being put into the position of the wife, and we had never played that game.

As I write this, I am unable to say whether Thomas and I are lovers or ex-lovers. Although we no longer live together, we still have meals and spend vacations together. I see or call him several times each day. We make all important decisions together. On the other hand, we do a number of things separately. We no longer sleep with each other. I am absorbed in the gay civil rights struggle; he is indifferent to it. Still, neither of us will ever be as close to another human being. We were in love once, passionately. I allowed my work to divide us. If I could choose again, I would subordinate my work to my relationship with Thomas. I realize now what I did not then: I was still convinced that homosexuality was a psychological disorder. It followed that achievements the straight world could approve of were more important than a love it condemned.

After I came out publicly, I became the most prominent self-confessed homosexual in America, partly because I was a member of a profession regarded as a citadel of respectability. (The noted novelist Merle Miller had very courageously come out publicly in 1971, but writers have never been regarded as models of morality or pillars of society.) Yet, of course, the achievements and fame of many homosexuals far exceed mine. It is unfortunate that these men, whose careers would dramatically illustrate how socially useful homosexuals can be, feel they must keep their sexual identity especially well hidden. I asked a number of homosexuals who hold high posts in city and state governments and in the federal government, as well as several well-known civil rights leaders, if they would describe for publication in this book the effects their homosexuality has had on their careers. To a man, they declined, fearing that their careers would be blasted and the projects to which they have given their lives discredited.

In the fields of law and religion, probably no more than a dozen men have helped—by publicly announcing their homosexuality—to shatter stereotypes and provide role models for young homosexuals. In medicine, the number of men who have come forward in this manner is just as small. There are some 334,000 doctors in this country. According to Kinsey's percentages, this would mean that 13,000 American doctors are exclusively homosexual, and another 20,000 or so are predominantly, though not exclusively, homosexual. But so far only about twenty doctors, most of them young, have publicly announced their homosexuality.

Let me add that I understand only too well why so few men dare to come out in public. But I am convinced that if several mature, respected homosexuals came forward and declared that they are "one of those," the effect would be to alter drastically and forever the public's attitude toward us and the attitude of homosexuals, young and old, toward themselves.

In the following pages I shall describe how their homosexuality has affected the careers of seven men—an insurance company officer, a neurosurgeon, the head of a research foundation, a male prostitute-turned-social worker, a New York City policeman, a mechanic, and a state legislator. It is quite a range of professions; their stories are similarly varied—from disaster on up.

Lloyd, at age fifty-three, had worked his way up from a door-to-door salesman for a large insurance company to the point where, in 1973, he was about to be promoted to a vice-presidency. The company was as top-heavy with Wasps and males as it could get away with in the face of laws prohibiting race and sex discrimination in hiring.

Ability and solidity—these were the qualities company officers looked for in their white, clean-cut, short-haired ranks. Lloyd was a homosexual who had been living for twelve years with a man he told neighbors and visitors was his cousin. In 1968 Lloyd's lover was crippled in an automobile accident and confined for the rest of his life to a wheelchair. Lloyd made him the beneficiary of his own life insurance policy, explaining to the company that he had an obligation to provide for a relative who was no longer able to work.

As part of a final check on the man they were about to promote, the senior officers of Lloyd's company sent an investigator to speak with Lloyd's neighbors and to interview people in his "cousin's" home town. The investigator used the standard ploy—the young man was about to become the beneficiary of an $80,000 insurance policy. His former neighbors talked freely, and the investigator soon learned that the man was in fact not related to Lloyd. Back in Lloyd's town, he learned that the two men had been living together for years. With the investigator's report in hand, the company officials called Lloyd in and demanded his immediate resignation. "The word 'homosexual' was not mentioned; they were too polite for that," Lloyd told me shortly before he and his lover moved to the West Coast, where Lloyd hoped to set up a small florist shop. Since then, neither I nor any of his other East Coast friends have heard from him.

Dr. Henry D. Messer, the neurosurgeon and one of the three men who helped me to come out publicly, is an officer of the Mattachine Society. A graduate of Duke University Medical School, Henry is director of neurosurgery at Harlem Hospital and on the staffs of St. Vincent's, Polyclinic, and Beekman Downtown hospitals. He might well have vanished from the professional horizon had he not been very determined and had a doctor not overlooked his homosexuality at a crucial moment in his career.

Shortly before he was to be discharged from the Air Force Medical Corps, in which he was serving as a surgeon, Henry's wallet was stolen from the officers' quarters. Unfortunately it contained his official identification papers as well as some money. Henry knew who the thief was and promptly reported the incident to the military authorities. When the thief was apprehended a few hours later, Henry's wallet was discovered in his pocket. He claimed that he had not stolen it, that Henry was a homosexual who had propositioned him, etc., etc. The Air Force dug deep, sending investigators to interrogate Henry's parents, the sheriff of his home town, and a number of his high school friends. Henry's address book was confiscated; it no doubt would not have been had it contained the addresses of women, married or unmarried. He was given the choice of standing a court-martial or resigning his commission under less than honorable conditions. Henry chose the latter and left the Air Force one month earlier than his scheduled separation date.

Henry had already been accepted as a resident for specialty training in surgery at a large New York City hospital. He decided that before starting his residency he would tell his chief of service he was homosexual. To Henry's astonishment, the surgeon had already been told. (Henry does not know to this day whether it was the Air Force that had informed on him or some helpful buddy.) In any event, his chief of service kept Henry on as a resident: It would have been difficult for him not to, Henry told me, since he would not have been able to find another resident with Henry's qualifications on such short notice. Four years later, having completed his residency and about to take the board exam in neurosurgery, he applied to the American College of Surgeons for membership. At this point, his "understanding" chief of service did an about-face. As Henry himself wrote, under a pseudonym, in a 1973 issue of *Medical Opinion,*

My chief of service, a well-meaning but misguided man who had used me as a resident for four years, apparently had a delayed guilt reaction for having "harbored" a homosexual. He decided that he must tell the truth for the good of all concerned. So he informed the ACS and my specialty board that I was homosexual. To their credit, the ACS approved my membership, making me an FACS [Fellow of the American College of Surgeons]. The specialty board, however, turned down my request to take the exam on the grounds of "poor moral character."

(I should explain that before the applicant can take this examination, he has to submit letters of character reference. Henry's chief of service had written the specialty board that *because* Henry was a homosexual he was of poor moral character and therefore not qualified to take the exam.)

Some years later Henry reapplied for permission to take the exam and was again denied it. His colleagues naturally wondered if Henry might be less capable than he seemed. There were very few doctor friends, gay or straight, to whom he felt close enough to explain the situation. This lack of formal certification meant that he might not be reappointed to his hospital, and, of course, without permission to operate at a hospital he could never practice. Finally, a new department chief at the hospital urged Henry to apply one last time to take the exam, explaining that a number of the board's more conservative members had either retired or died. At last his request was granted, and he passed with flying colors.

But Henry Messer's career as a board-certified neurosurgeon had been delayed ten years. No wonder he is an activist in the fight for gay civil rights.

Society's attitude toward homosexuality does not always destroy careers, as it did the insurance official's, or nearly destroy them, as it did Henry Messer's; it very often only undermines a man's conviction of his own authority and worth. Unable to believe that he will ever be loved or, as in my own case with Thomas, unable to believe in the value of this love, the homosexual may substitute achievement for affection—and with a vengeance. Obviously, heterosexual men are not immune to this malady. Many use their work as a means of hiding from their wives and children and, hooked on their own careers, grow increasingly remote from them. At the same time, every hierarchy appears both to attract vacuum-packed men and to encourage the production of more. Men who consider their own thoughts and feelings insignificant, or do not even know what they think and feel, make good servants. And even in the land of the free there is always an opening for a smart slave. During the Watergate summer of 1973, how many upwardly mobile, inwardly hollow men were paraded before our eyes—a whole chain gang of command.

Cecil is the fifty-six-year-old head of an important research foundation and a homosexual who has never known a loving relationship with another human being. I had known Cecil for nearly twenty years without ever suspecting that he was homosexual.

A few days before I came out publicly, I decided to tell four or five of my closest straight friends so that they would not have to find out about me from the newspapers. I asked Cecil to come to my home, and after the second round of drinks, I said: "We've known each other a long time, and there's something I want you to know. I'm a homosexual, and in a couple of days I'm going to announce it publicly." Cecil looked at me for a long while without saying a word; then he said, "Howard, don't you know that I'm homosexual?" As I say, I hadn't had a clue.

After he left, I searched my memory for the clues I had obviously overlooked. I recalled that he had visited me at St. Vincent's both times I was hospitalized (for hepatitis and for my heart attack). Each time there had been gay visitors in the room, young doctors just out of their specialty training, not the sort of doctors I would normally know. I had quickly introduced Cecil in terms of his professional position, which was a way of saying, "Careful, he's straight." Both times, he had surprised me by staying so long and saying so little, and he had never said a word about the presence of those young men.

There was also the classic clue: He was single. But then, I knew a number of straight single men, some divorced, others bachelors, who led lives almost as sexually promiscuous as Thomas's. Cecil was simply a man whose sexual preference I had just not ever stopped to wonder about. As head of a health research foundation, he had been helpful in many ways when I was with HIP and, later, with Gouverneur; and when I was health services administrator, I was glad to be able to lend support to a number of his projects. I respected his judgment so much that I often discussed changes in my professional life with him, as well as crucial health care matters. On occasion, we would get together for drinks and dinner. Now I see that he never left an opening for personal conversation. He always gave the impression that it was health causes that were on his mind. He was, in a word, impersonal. I supposed that he spent his evenings with others as he did with me, talking about work.

Recently, Cecil told me about the experiences that had hollowed him out emotionally, leaving a void that only work could fill. Our conversation was the first time he had attempted to talk about himself to someone other than a psychiatrist.

"I've lived most of my life in terror," he began. "Terror

of my dictatorial mother, then terror of the constant fights between her and my father, but most of all terror of my homosexuality. I was six or seven when I realized that my feelings about other boys were not what is considered normal. And I was bookish rather than athletic. From the third grade on, other children called me a fairy.

"I had my first sexual experience when I was thirteen. It was with my uncle, who was living with us then. It was a small house, and the two of us had to share a double bed. One night, thinking that I was asleep, he began to stroke and fondle me. I was terrified and intrigued at the same time. This continued throughout my high school years. I usually pretended to be sound asleep. The sex was always pleasing.

"It was only when I began to sleep with a high school friend that it dawned on me I might be homosexual. It wasn't so much that with him I was willing and active rather than passive as with my uncle, as that he forced me to realize how frightened I was of having sex with girls. One night, when my parents and my uncle were away, he brought two girls to my house. One was for him, the other for me. He wanted to initiate me, to get me laid. I ran out of the room.

"I had sexual relationships with two other boys in high school. They are both now married and have children. I continued to sleep with one of them right through college and into the early years of his marriage. But we were never really lovers except technically—I mean, there wasn't very much affection.

"And that was it, until just two years ago. Until 1972, nothing—nothing but suppressing my feelings, nothing but living in isolation and terror. And all the time I kept thinking to myself: I'm not really homosexual, it's something I'll outgrow.

"As my emotional life shriveled, my professional career

grew and grew until it assumed the proportions of a skyscraper that had been built next door to a hovel.

"A few years after I became the head [of the research foundation] I had an emotional upheaval. I really did not know what was wrong, but I knew that something was badly interfering with my life. I consulted a physician, who referred me to a psychiatrist. One Friday afternoon I went to this psychiatrist, who told me that I was having a nervous breakdown. He gave me electric shock treatment —in his office, that very afternoon. A physician friend took me home and I was able to get to sleep with the help of a sedative he gave me. I was back at work on Monday, not having missed a single day.

"After that, I saw another psychiatrist—for nine years, until 1972. I thought he could cure me of my homosexuality. I came to realize there was no cure.

"Toward the end of my therapy, a brilliant associate on my staff—a young man I had hired myself—suddenly and with great emotion told me he was homosexual. He told me about all his lovers and his sexual experiences. I found myself telling him about my uncle and my three high school friends—it was all I had to tell about.

"That was two years ago. Since that evening, for some reason I have turned more and more away from heterosexual friends, colleagues, associates. Now I avoid all those dinners, cocktail parties, and so on. But shunning the society of heterosexuals has, of course, only increased my loneliness.

"I suppose you could say that at the age of fifty-six, I am beginning to understand my homosexuality. I do not know where I will go from here. I will certainly never come out publicly. I would not tarnish the foundation in any way. All I know is that I have a lot of emotional catching up to do. Yet after all these years of deprivation and loneliness and fear and hiding from myself, I suppose it is unrealistic to think that I will ever catch up."

158

For ten years Henry Messer's career was blocked or threatened by someone's discovering he was homosexual. For more than twice that length of time Cecil's personal life was blighted by fears and guilts instilled in him by society's attitude toward homosexuality.

Cliff, on the other hand, made a career out of his homosexuality. He started hustling, or working as a male prostitute, when he was fifteen. Now, at twenty-six, he is in the second year of a program that will earn him his master's degree in social work. The program involves working with a counseling agency under the supervision of an experienced social worker. Cliff is getting his practical experience by serving in a New York counseling center for homosexuals. I'm on the board of that center, which is how I came to know him.

"I knew I was gay when I was eleven or twelve," he told me, "and as soon as I knew, I felt guilty. I come from a middle-class background and I was taught to feel guilty about everything connected with sex, and though I never asked, I knew that being gay was the worst sin in the book. So I quickly learned all the tricks you can use to hide it— what to say, how to react, to be good at sports, to look straight. Knowing I could fool people made me feel strong, but at the same time the guilt made me suffer.

"I had just turned fifteen when I came out—in Times Square. I waited around, and finally this man approached me. I was so terrified I couldn't even speak, but I knew that I wanted to go with him. My body kept telling me I had to have it. And he offered me twenty dollars. I was so young and so dumb that I just thought, 'Well, if you're gay, that's the way it's done.' I had dreamed of having sex with a man for years, but this was the first time. Well, when he offered me the money, I couldn't get any words to come out of my mouth, so I had to shake my head yes.

"I had come uptown for sex, and the first man who

picked me up had paid me, so that was my first experience as a hustler. I wasn't very good. I was interested in affection and all he wanted was sex, and I didn't know the first thing about who did what and what went where. Afterward, I remember, I felt terribly guilty. I saw what I had done as an irreversible act. The only way I could ease my guilt was to put that twenty-dollar bill in a can for some cancer drive.

"The next day I felt guilty, but I wanted to have sex again, so I went back to Forty-second Street. And each time I went back somebody would approach me and ask me if I would go home with him for a certain amount of money, and half the time I would keep the money and half the time I would stuff it into a cancer can.

"I kept this up for a few months because I still thought this was what life had to be like if you were gay. But after a while it started to hit me. I realized that not all homosexuals pay or get paid, and I started to feel the double guilt of being both a prostitute and a homosexual. Still, I really didn't know what else to do; besides, I was beginning to like some of the men who paid me.

"I began to meet nicer men when I got off Times Square and started cruising the lobbies of hotels like the Americana or the Plaza. In the hotels I met businessmen who were in town for a weekend or a week and didn't know anybody. They usually wanted to see me several times during their week, and sometimes they took me out to dinner and a show. And when I was free during the day—because this was going on while I was still in high school—I sometimes took them to my favorite spots, like the top of the Empire State Building or the Statue of Liberty."

After he had been hustling on his own for several months, someone put Cliff in touch with a "call-boy service."

"Working for a service was really funny, when you stop to think about it," Cliff said. "In school I was incredibly active in extracurricular activities, like the drama guild and the student government, and I was an officer of several of them. I was really very looked up to in school. After school I would go home and have dinner with my family, and then I'd do some homework, and when I was done with my homework, at around eight or nine, I would call up this guy who ran the service and he would give me the name of my trick for the evening. And I would go out and take care of him. My boss used to insist that we go out at least four nights a week. In time I built up a regular clientele. Men would ask specifically for me.

"I guess there were about twenty of us in that service; most of them were in their early twenties, but a few—five or six, maybe—were still in high school. Some of them had to work every night to support a habit. That was the one thing that really turned me off about this operation. The guy who ran it was a dealer, and he got kids hooked on drugs. This whole experience set me so violently against drugs that I now have a psychological block against taking even something as mild as aspirin."

Cliff worked for the service for two years. "I can remember seeing *Irma La Douce*," he said, "and feeling, 'That's me.' I got involved with everyone. Part of it was that I was lonely, and the men I met were lonely, too—lonely in the sense that they didn't have any gay friends." Many of his clients were married, Cliff said, most were successful businessmen, and a few were celebrities. "But they had nobody they could confide in that they were gay. Their loneliness was the loneliness that comes from always being with straight people." A number of his clients told Cliff that they had not had sex for five or six years.

The part of his job he enjoyed the most was discovering his client's sexual fantasies. "After a while," Cliff said, "even the most inhibited people would share their inner-most fantasies with me. Sometimes we'd even work them up into a scenario and play them out. I might get dressed and go outside and come back five minutes later pretending I was a newsboy coming to deliver a paper. Depending on what we had decided beforehand, I would start to seduce him or he would start to seduce me, offering me a drink, making small talk, then getting suggestive, and so on until, like with one guy, we were both completely naked and nothing ever happened. But sometimes their fantasy was rape, and then I would leave and knock on the door a few minutes later and he would open it and grab me, and it would be very violent. Getting them to reveal their fantasies was like a game."

When he was seventeen, Cliff began to see a psychiatrist regularly. His analyst, unlike mine, did not regard homo-sexuality as a psychic ailment, but as a way of life made traumatic by society's attitude toward it. "It was through analysis," Cliff told me, "that I started to feel positive about my homosexuality, and suddenly I realized that a lot of my knowledge of people and of the world was due to my being gay and being a hustler."

At nineteen, still in analysis and now a free-lance male prostitute with a regular clientele, Cliff enrolled in a college in New York City, intending to major in drama. That was in 1969, the year of the Stonewall riots. Two years later, Cliff took part in his first gay activist demon-stration. "All of a sudden, all that political bullshit I'd read for years became relevant to me. I saw how the laws this society had made were responsible for most of the guilt I'd felt most of my life and for a lot of the damage done to those middle-aged men I was seeing. I saw how we'd all been manipulated, and it seemed to me that the only way we could change things was to get out there and fight to get sensible laws passed and the nonsensical ones repealed."

Cliff joined the Gay Activists Alliance, where he met a different sort of homosexual from those he had encountered as a hustler—gay psychologists and gay social workers among them. Through his work with the GAA, Cliff found new direction for his life—a desire to help other gay people. In the fall of 1973 he dropped his theater program and started on his master's degree in social work.

While preparing to make this shift, Cliff, under the supervision of a gay social worker, occasionally served at GAA headquarters as a peer counselor—a counselor who draws upon his own life experience for guidance. The social worker told me that Cliff had succeeded in "getting to several very troubled young homosexuals who had remained closed and uncooperative" in sessions with more experienced counselors. The social worker was impressed by Cliff's skill at improvising solutions to problems that had stumped others. One recurrent problem among the homosexuals Cliff counseled was their inability to find jobs. Cliff and a colleague had the bright idea of setting up a gay employment service.

Now, in their spare time, the two men try to find jobs for the thirty or so homosexuals who come into their office every week. Cliff and his partner face an uphill struggle trying to place these homosexuals who tend to be effeminate, the kind of person regular employment agencies refuse to assist. "Other agencies," Cliff said, "tell them they have nothing for them, which is a lie. Blacks used to get the same runaround all the time. I know people in these agencies, and they've told me that almost all personnel or placement agencies stamp a number or a letter on their applications that means 'gay,' and virtually unplaceable. It's against the law, but they do it anyway. Even if they only suspect that a man is gay, they'll put the number or letter on his form. The agencies feel that it will reflect poorly on them if they send a homosexual to an employer who has trusted them for years. So sometimes we call up a gay employee or a sympathetic straight at one of those agencies and ask him to help us out. Surprisingly often, he does."

Boys whose parents have driven them from their homes on discovering that they are homosexual repeatedly turn up at the agency. Cliff and his partner find them temporary living quarters, then try to find them jobs. The majority of the boys have no skills—a problem Cliff and his partner are attempting to solve by setting up special listings of openings for jobs as waiters, dishwashers, messenger boys, and the like.

For a young man who started out as a bewildered hustler on Times Square, Cliff has already come a long way and has helped an impressive number of troubled homosexuals.

Officer O'Neill, as I'll call him, of the New York City Police, is a homosexual who discovered his sexual identity only after he had joined the force. One dramatic afternoon, his private life and police career unexpectedly merged—or collided—when he was sent out to break up a group of gay civil rights activists and found himself confronted by an angry young man who knew that he, O'Neill, was gay, too.

O'Neill's case is probably not as unique as it sounds. I have known a number of gay policemen, and I suspect that most of them, at some point in their careers, have been called upon to arrest homosexuals.

O'Neill is forty-four, the son of Irish immigrants and the first member of his family to graduate from high school. He joined the police force shortly after serving in Korea, where he had seen plenty of action. Two years after joining the force, he married a girl from County Clare with whom he had four children in as many years. He and his wife were, and are, devout Catholics. On the job, he won several citations for bravery. His personal life, however, was complicated by his discovery, five years after his marriage, that he was homosexual.

O'Neill had known for some time that something was missing in his marriage. He could satisfy his wife sexually, but not himself. He rejected the idea that he might be homosexual. As an adolescent he had engaged in sex play with other boys, but so had almost all the other kids in the neighborhood, and they had since gone straight and married. Then, too, O'Neill thought homosexuals had to be effeminate, and he was muscular and stocky. Like most of us at this stage, he regarded himself as an enigma into which he had better not pry too deeply. But, almost against his will, he began to hang out with members of the morals squad in order to watch how they entrapped homosexuals. (This was in the early sixties when the police were arresting large numbers of homosexuals.) The usual tactic was to post a handsome young plainclothesman as a lure at one end of a block and another plainclothesman some thirty yards farther on, and to arrest the passing homosexual the moment he responded to the lure. O'Neill learned two things from his observations: that not all homosexuals are effeminate, and how to make a pickup.

One evening in 1963, O'Neill set out to entrap a homosexual, planning, he says, to make an arrest if he were propositioned. It seems clear that O'Neill was really testing himself. He could always arrest the man at the last moment if he felt he could not go through with the sex; or he could sleep with the man and not mention that he was a policeman. O'Neill took up his post on a well-known pickup thoroughfare and was duly propositioned. He found that he liked the young man. Furthermore, he found that sex with a man gave him far more satisfaction than sex with a woman ever had. From that moment on, O'Neill considered himself homosexual.

He thought of resigning from the force, but he knew

of no other way to earn a living, and he had a wife and four children to support. If, however, his homosexuality weighed on his conscience as a policeman who in the line of duty would be expected to arrest homosexuals, it also helped him to solve a domestic problem that had been troubling him for some time. He and his wife had decided not to have any more children. As devout Catholics, however, they could not use contraceptives. His wife had wanted to give up intercourse. But O'Neill required some sort of sex life, and also felt obliged to continue playing the role of the sexually aggressive male. Now, with one need satisfied and the other eliminated, he could stop pretending.

He resumed his pickup tactics and in time made friends with a number of homosexuals, a few of whom he told he was a police officer. Then, in 1965, he fell in love with a young man he had met on the street. He never seriously considered divorcing his wife. As a Catholic he did not countenance divorce. He was devoted to his children, and feared that if he were to divorce his wife he might be denied visitation rights. Furthermore, his marriage was a good cover. He did, however, move out and set up house with his lover in a small apartment on Manhattan's West Side. Everything was going very well, from his point of view. Then came the day that he will never be able to forget.

It was the day on which the general welfare committee of the New York City Council was to vote on an anti-discrimination bill for homosexuals. Outside the council chamber, a large crowd of gay activists had gathered to await the outcome. Most of them were young—students or men who worked at part-time jobs or were on welfare, the bold kind that agitated in public while older homosexuals like me clung to do-nothing privacy. The general welfare committee had failed to vote the bill out of

166

committee shortly before, despite intense lobbying on the part of the activists. Now the activists were sure that they had mustered enough support to get the bill out of committee and have it voted into law by the council.

Hours passed. The activists waited. Finally the door of the council chamber opened and the committee members filed out. Once again the measure to vote the bill out of committee had been defeated. The activists were stunned. Fifteen of them ran out of City Hall and across the park, toward the Brooklyn Bridge. It was late afternoon, the beginning of the rush hour. The fifteen young men lay down across the western approach lanes to the bridge and, as a gesture of solidarity and defiance, held hands to form a chain, chanting "Gay is proud."

Officer O'Neill was one of the policemen dispatched to break the chain that was blocking traffic on the bridge. When he set out, he had not been told who the protesters were or what it was they were protesting. At the bridge, the honks of the hundreds of blocked cars drowned out the protesters' chants. It was not until O'Neill and his men had worked their way up close to the human chain that he heard the chant "Gay is proud" and, looking down, saw a face he recognized. The young college student in the middle of the chain was the lover of a friend of his. They had met many times. O'Neill stared, terrified. He had already given his orders: The protesters were to be picked up and carried to the police vans. But it was taking time to pry the young men's hands apart, and the protesters were shouting "pig" and "son of a bitch." The man he knew was looking directly at him, shouting "pig" and "fink." O'Neill could hardly move; he wondered when the young man would add "queer" and "cocksucker." He had more time to wonder than he had hoped—the young man was the last of the fifteen to be picked up and carried off.

Back at the station, O'Neill was in a panic. He knew

that under normal circumstances a gay person would never reveal another to a straight person. But he also knew that his career and his livelihood were at stake, and the young demonstrator had been very angry. Would the rule still apply in the case of a gay cop who had just arrested homosexuals for staging a protest for gay civil rights—his own civil rights?

O'Neill did not know what to do. He knew none of the leaders of the gay movement and so could not ask their help. Then he thought of me. We had met some months before at a party, and he remembered that I had been trying to raise money for the Gay Activists Alliance; perhaps *I* could somehow save him. He ran out of the station house and called me from a phone booth. By this time he was practically sobbing. I assured him that the young man would never tell other policemen about him. My assurances were not enough. He begged me to call the GAA and ask them to make certain that none of the protesters would talk. I did. None of the protesters had even thought of informing on him. Officer O'Neill's reputation was safe.

For several months after this incident, O'Neill, although still living with his lover, denied to other homosexuals that he was exclusively gay. He claimed that he was bisexual and that his marriage proved it. O'Neill has since abandoned this frail line of defense against his renewed fears of exposure. Now he makes no secret of his homosexuality—among other homosexuals, that is. On the force, he remains indistinguishable from his fellow officers except, perhaps, for his bravery, for which he continues to receive citations.

Not all homosexuals have gone through experiences as traumatic as O'Neill's. Nor is homosexuality always a hindrance to one's career, as Cliff's case shows and as the case of my friend Cecil tangentially shows. While some highly placed homosexuals discriminate against other homosexuals in order to prevent rumors that could endanger their own positions, most do what they can to help one another. To judge by what I have seen of it, this underground placement service works only for qualified candidates. No one wants to recommend a dud. And since homosexuals are apt to feel less secure in their jobs than their heterosexual counterparts, they tend to be particularly careful about the people they recommend.

In recent years, there appears to have been a slight lessening of public hostility toward homosexuals, at least in and around some big cities and college towns. The on-the-job experience of the New Jersey mechanic whom I met at the GAA meeting in Hackensack in the fall of 1973 is an interesting, if ambiguous, case in point.

Larry, as I'll call him, is a divorced father of three who recently came out as a homosexual. I asked him how the other mechanics in his shop had reacted.

"Well," he said, "I'd been working at the shop for a couple of years, and the guys all knew me and they'd never thought of me as gay. So when I came out, they didn't know what to expect. Would I come in wearing a dress? That's the kind of crack I got, because they thought—the way *I* used to—that a queer was a guy who went around in women's clothes or something. They looked at me, and I wasn't any different. So they got used to it. Except nobody will go into the john now when I'm using it."

"Do the men in the shop ever talk to you about homosexuality?" I asked.

"Oh, they kid me about it sometimes, but that's as far as it goes—though it kind of gets to me that whenever they want to put somebody down they call him a cocksucker. I told them to lay off, so now they do it even more. But the way they talk about women is worse. People should just be people."

Larry has lived for two years with a young window

dresser named Nicky. I asked him if he ever brought Nicky to work.

"Sure."

"How do the men at the shop react to him?"

"Very good. They think I'm the husband and Nicky's the wife, since he's a window dresser. They're much nicer to him than they are to me. Sometimes he helps out around the shop, and if he drops a wrench or something they pick it up for him, even though he could do it himself. I guess they think a window dresser is supposed to be gay but a mechanic isn't. Sometimes they'll see me looking at some guy and say, 'Hey, what about Nicky?' And I say I hope he's looking at someone nice, too. Then they say I better not cheat on my wife. But I tell them it's not cheating, and Nicky is not my wife. If I go out with someone else I tell Nicky about it, and if he goes out with someone else he tells me. I hope he has a good time, and he hopes I have a good time. They can't figure that one out. It's just what *they* would like to do, but they flip when they hear that anybody is actually doing it."

Larry doubts that he would have been kept on at the large dealership he works for if he had been a salesman instead of a mechanic. In the shop he can wear his Lambda button on his overalls, but most employers will not tolerate any visible sign of homosexuality in those who represent their company to the public. It's "bad for the business."

One might also assume that even a hint of homosexuality would be enough to destroy a politician's reputation. But the case of state legislator Allan H. Spear shows that this is not necessarily so.

Spear is a thirty-five-year-old state senator from Minnesota who makes no secret of the fact that he is homosexual. Like Larry, he openly wears a Lambda button.

Spear is also a history professor and the author of a

respected book on the history of black Americans. Born in the Midwest and educated in the Ivy League, he became involved in the black civil rights movement in the mid-fifties. More recently he has helped to organize white groups in his community to support the Black Panthers and Chicano farm workers, and he has worked to raise money to help pay for the defense of the Indians who fought at Wounded Knee. It was only in 1972, the year he ran for a seat in the state legislature, that Spear realized that "I had been fighting for everybody's cause except my own" and began to actively support gay liberation. Spear's coming out as a homosexual and his emergence as a candidate for public office coincided—a coincidence that seemed certain to be devastating to his new career but that tellingly proved not to be.

How is it that a civil-rights-minded, politically active homosexual was so slow to identify himself with a cause so close to home?

Spear was fourteen when he realized that he was homosexual, twenty when he had his first homosexual experiences—infrequent pickups on Chicago street corners. "What I saw," he told me, "was the street-corner scene and a bit of the bar scene, and they turned me off. There was nobody I could identify with. I was career-minded and properly ambitious and respectable, and I wanted out."

Spear started seeing a psychiatrist when he was twenty-four and doing graduate work in history at Yale. "I walked in and said to the shrink, 'Here I am. I'm homosexual, and I want you to cure me.' I went to him for about a year, and his approach was that my real problem wasn't that I was queer, since I hadn't had any homosexual life since Chicago, but that I was unable to relate to women. 'You relate to people too intellectually; you are unable to relate to them emotionally, unable to let down your guard—especially with women. Why don't you try relating to women? Why don't you try letting those barriers down? Those homosexual fantasies of yours will go away then.' They didn't, of course."

Relying on a traditional remedy, Spear became, as he put it, "the world's best sublimator," a grind set on finishing his dissertation as quickly as possible and finding a job. He received his doctorate in history in 1965 and was promptly offered a job at the University of Minnesota, where he has remained ever since, except when on leave as a visiting professor.

What moved Spear, a white who grew up in a predominantly white town, to specialize in the history of blacks? He says that his homosexuality had a good deal to do with it. "Being gay, I've always felt alienated, an outsider in our society, and in the fifties the blacks were the most visible outsiders in our society. I got involved in black history in graduate school because of my undergraduate activities in the civil rights movement. One interest led naturally to the other. Amazingly, I had been fascinated by minorities for years before I realized that I belonged to one myself."

During his first years as a professor, he continued to sublimate his sexual urges in his work—preparing his courses, lecturing, writing a book, getting it published, pushing for a promotion—and in his extracurricular liberal-cause activities. Up until about 1967, he says, "I had virtually no sex life at all. Occasionally, if I was out of town, at a convention or something, I'd go to a gay bar, but I did nothing in my own city. I didn't know a single gay person there. All my friends were straight, or at least I assumed they were, and they assumed I was."

Then Spear met a woman, who also assumed that he was straight, and for a time convinced him that perhaps he was. Spear warned her that he had never had a full relationship with a woman—which was as close as he could come to saying he was gay. But she was not to be deterred, and a few weeks after they met, they went to bed together. To Spear's astonishment, he found that he enjoyed making love with a woman. The relationship did not last, however: When the issue of marriage inevitably arose, both of them backed off.

Two years later, in 1969, Spear served as visiting professor at a West Coast university and for the first time in many years began to lead an actively homosexual life. Back in Minnesota, however, he resumed the straight (or largely neuter) existence of previous years. It was not until the spring of 1972, when delegates were being elected to the National Democratic Convention, that he began to face up to the political implications of homosexuality and finally to come out.

Spear had long been active within the Democratic party. He had waged a campaign to be elected a delegate to the party convention, and his nomination appeared secure. When a member of the local gay caucus announced that he, too, would run for a delegate's seat, Spear's political associates were annoyed. They saw the need for blacks and Chicanos on the state delegation, but homosexuals? The general reaction was: What's the big deal about being gay? So somebody comes along and says he's gay and tries to rip off a state delegate spot—who needs that? Spear was disturbed. He had worked for blacks and Chicanos for years; now he saw that they, along with the rest of the rank and file of party workers, regarded gay civil rights as trivial. The professor's growing sympathy for the gay caucus cause turned to terror, however, when the gay candidate asked Spear if he would mind answering questions from the floor regarding his attitude toward homosexuals. Spear took this as a sign that the caucus knew he was gay, resented his hiding it, and was merely going to embarrass him into withdrawing his name. Later he spoke privately with members of the gay caucus and found that this had not been their intention. He also found the group attractive and stimulating. At a meeting that day, members had stood up one by one and said that they were proud of being gay. He wanted to be like them but felt that he had lived the pseudo-straight life too long to change his ways now.

Still, if he could not announce his homosexuality to the assembled state party members, he could at least ease his mind by telling a few members of the gay caucus. The first member he confided in asked Spear if he knew other homosexuals in town. The man then asked if he were interested in meeting others. When Spear said yes, his new friend promptly took him downtown for his first visit to a local gay bar, where he met a man he had worked with on a number of projects without ever suspecting that the man was gay. From that night on, "things started rolling," Spear told me. "The more gay people I met, the more I wanted to meet others and the more I wanted to identify myself with them and their cause. And then I felt, 'Well, why can't I start telling my straight friends, too?' "

The first time was difficult. Few heterosexuals can imagine how hard it is for a man, particularly a man Spear's age or older, to tell straight friends whom he has known for years that he is a homosexual. "Intellectually, I knew that my friends wouldn't turn against me when I told them, but in the back of my mind I still felt that my whole world would fall apart. The need to conceal my homosexuality had been such a part of me for so long that I couldn't imagine living without it. After all, a lot of my life had been built around keeping that secret."

Spear's world did not fall in on him. The first two straight friends he told—a married couple—proved sympathetic. In fact, he found that his openness deepened his friendship with the couple. "It was the first time I had ever talked about myself, my feelings, me. We had always talked about politics, causes, things like that. The result was that they opened up about themselves and their feelings. We had been close friends, but now we became even closer."

Spear then invited a number of straight friends to what he was later to regard as "an almost comical series of melodramatic little dinner parties." Each guest in turn would be served supper and then, "somewhere between dessert and coffee," Spear would spring his confession on him. He says that he gave a dozen such surprise parties before deciding that enough was enough. He did not pledge any of his guests to secrecy, though he did tell them he hoped the news wouldn't appear in the next issue of the local paper.

The professor's confessional spring of '72 led up to a politically surprising June. That month, the state supreme court issued a reapportionment plan that created in the city a new, very liberal district—it encompassed the university community—without an incumbent. Spear was one of the best-known liberal Democrats in the district; his friends urged him to run. The following exchange, he says, was typical:

Spear:   Look, you're asking me to run for office just as I'm starting to come out as a homosexual. This is a terrible time for me to run for office.

Friends:   How would you handle the homosexual angle if you did run?

Spear:   Well, the first thing is, I'm not going back into the closet. I'm happy, I'm even exhilarated by having come out and gotten to know other homosexuals. I feel freer than I've ever felt in my life. And I'm just not going to go back.

Friends:   Does that mean you're going to run as a homo-

175

sexual candidate? Because if it does, you're not going to win.

Spear: No, I'm going to run as a liberal candidate, but at the same time I'm going to include the gay issue with the other issues. And if anyone asks me if I'm gay, I am not going to deny it.

Friends: That's fair enough.

During the campaign, Spear says, rumors about his being a homosexual circulated through his district, and he is sure that his opponent knew that he was gay. But the rumors did not lead to direct questions, and his opponent did not exploit the rumors or in any way make an issue of homosexuality. Spear won the November election by a comfortable margin.

How many of his constituents, his party associates, and his fellow legislators know that Spear is a homosexual?* When I visited him recently in Minnesota, he maintained that "anyone with two eyes and two ears" should know, since he has closely identified himself with the gay movement, is often seen with known gay people, and wears the Lambda button. Most of his political associates know. Each year a group of about a dozen of his political friends spend a weekend together at a state park. Last year Spear asked if he could bring along the man he was seeing at the time and was told that of course he could. "We were five straight couples and my friend and me," he told me. "We sat by the fire at night, and they held hands and we held hands, and they went off to bed together and we went off to bed together. Afterward I asked one couple how the others had reacted. Had there been a lot of talk? They told me—and I believe them—that nobody had raised an eyebrow or said a word."

The majority leader of the senate has tactfully revealed

* Since the writing of this book, Spear has come out publicly.

176

that he knows Spear is homosexual. "And if he knows," Spear said, "then most people in the legislature probably do, too." Spear occasionally discusses the issue of gay rights with his colleagues in the senate—a gay rights bill was recently voted down in his state. In such discussions, Spear remarked, "my homosexuality never comes up. We talk about gay rights the same way we talk about any other issue, and that's just the way it should be."

I asked Spear if his involvement in the gay movement had altered his perceptions as a scholar with a special interest in minority groups. "When I took my first steps toward coming out a couple of years back," he replied, "I began to understand, on an emotional level, for the first time really, what black people go through when they 'get religion' in the sense of finding their identity, their wholeness as a people. I was working with local Afro-American prisoners, for example, and I saw that when they came to prison they started to read—Malcolm X, William DuBois, Richard Wright, Eldridge Cleaver, all the major black writers. And they got involved in black culture groups. Some of them became Black Muslims, some of them Panthers. Through these groups they came to understand what had happened to them as a people. They saw through the system that had kept them down, that had deprived them of the sense of their own worth. It's really hard for an outsider to comprehend the tremendous sense of liberation some of these men feel when they grasp what their people have been forced to endure and how the system has worked them over. I mean, here are people who felt born to failure suddenly realizing they were not born to fail but rather have been sentenced by this society to fail, and refusing to remain what it's made them."

The case of State Senator Allan Spear is hardly proof that the way is now open for homosexual politicians in America to pursue their careers without fear of their homosexuality being discovered and used against them. Spear's opponent did not resort to slurs, and Spear's constituency happens to be exceptionally well-educated and tolerant. And though Spear wears his Lambda button in public, he has been associated with so many civil rights causes for so long that his background provides a kind of cumulative camouflage for him in his present position. After all, if as a white man he could speak out for blacks, Chicanos, and Indians, he might equally well be a heterosexual speaking out for homosexuals.

The most hopeful conclusion to be drawn is that a homosexual who does not go out of his way to conceal his sexual identity can be elected by a sophisticated electorate —if, like Spear, he strikes the voters as a man who can do the job. And that, of course, is all that homosexuals are after: to be hired or fired, voted in or defeated, not on the basis of their sexual preference, but on their merits.

CHAPTER TEN

# Religion

As a young man I thought of myself as deeply religious. Almost all the members of my family to whom I felt close—my mother, my aunts, my paternal grandfather—were active churchgoers. My mother and aunts were Methodists, and I attended church regularly with them. When I visited my paternal grandfather, who was a Baptist, on his farm outside town, I went to church with him. A farmer who was interested in politics and became county commissioner, he was charitable, loving, and well-read, in notable contrast to my father and uncles, who regarded religion, book-learning, and all expressions of affection as fit only for women. "Real" men went hunting, watched ball games, and made money. My father and uncles' rejection of the church posed no particular problem for me, since I had rejected their values for those of my mother and grandfather. I accepted my grandfather as the model for my personal life; during high school I was a leader in the Epworth League, the Methodist youth organization.

All through my troubled adolescence, the church was a sustaining force in many ways. One did not have to be a good athlete to be a Christian; one could simply be a devout believer and try to do good and love one's neighbor as one's self. And one could pray to God for help and forgiveness. During my first year in college I regularly attended the Sunday service and the twice-weekly chapel service.

All this changed when I began to realize I was homosexual. I didn't exactly sit down and conclude that because I was homosexual, or had homosexual urges, I could not continue to be a Christian. Rather, the effect of my discovery of my sexual identity was subtle and all-pervading. Being homosexual, or whatever I was, seemed to put me in a world that was completely apart from the church. All the small-town and country churches I had grown up knowing emphasized the conventional rules of morality and revolved around the family. The Holy Family provided a model for us all. There was clearly no room for a homosexual in the church.

I felt that I was a sinner, condemned beyond all hope of salvation. Had I been familiar with the Catholic tradition of celibacy, I might have consoled myself for a time with the thought that theologians distinguish between being homosexual, which they say is not a sin, and engaging in homosexual acts, which they say is. In college, however, I did not worry so much about the afterlife as about what society would do to me if I acted on the sexual urges that kept returning with such intensity. I was not sure that I could make my way through this world, and the possibility that I could make my way into another world by being chaste was too remote to concern me.

I tried prayer, but not, as I recall, with much hope. Accepting the beliefs of the churchgoers I had known in my youth, I took it for granted that God would not stoop to help a queer. At the same time, I had no confidence that any of His ministers would be more helpful. I was already trying to do what I felt certain they would tell me I must do: give up my desire for men. Love, I knew, was the essence of Christian belief, and I knew, too, that "mercy triumphs over judgment," but I did not believe that Christian love and mercy could extend to me. I remember thinking that there were certain sins, certain kinds of immoral behavior, such as adultery, which society and the church did forgive, but not homosexuality—particularly when, as I was beginning to understand about myself, it was a central part of one's being. Forgiveness would have had to be a daily event.

Gradually I exchanged my belief in religion for a belief in science, in which I then included psychiatry. Where God and His ministers had failed, psychiatry and its practitioners seemed to hold out some hope for me. Psychiatrists would not judge and condemn, but, rather, listen and understand and heal. I was pretty naïve in those days.

Psychiatry used a different terminology from that of religion to condemn me, but the condemnation was just as devastating. I was no longer a sinner, but a psychopathic inferior and moral defective. In the later stages of therapy I was privileged to learn that, as a homosexual, I was narcissistic and incapable of love. If love was the ultimate human good, and one could never love, then one was doomed to a hell in this life. I certainly felt I was.

My early years in New York, during which I met men in gay bars and usually had only fleeting and impersonal sex with them, reinforced this sense of my being inherently immoral. When I found that there were homosexuals who could love and be loved, this sense of moral inferiority began to lessen. But it took me a long time, much too long, to understand what my real sins were: not having the homosexual feelings, but, as a consequence of trying to deny such feelings, rejecting many of the men who needed my concern and affection. I had no sympathy for men who

181

were weak or immature or narcissistic. Without really knowing it, I was being as judgmental as the church.

Condemned by the church and by psychiatry alike, I struggled to understand where, if anywhere, I and other homosexuals fit in the moral scheme of things. I was struck by an observation made by Reinhold Niebuhr, the theologian I admired most, concerning man's need to live for something beyond his immediate needs—the transcendental margin, he called it. I felt this need, and I discovered that I could fulfill it through serving causes such as improving health care for the poor. This provided me with some sense of my own worth, but it did little to help me accept my homosexuality. A long-time victim of clichés, I readily gave in to the notion that we homosexuals were generally attracted to professions that catered to narcissists: We were hairdressers, dress designers, interior decorators. The homosexuals who, I discovered, were at all levels of all the service professions and civil rights groups, I wrote off as anomalies. It took the establishment of gay service organizations and gay churches in the late 1960's and the early 1970's to shatter this cliché's powerful hold on me. These new service organizations and churches gave homosexuality a moral sanction. At the same time, they proved to me what I had been unpardonably slow to learn—that we, like others, are what we make of ourselves, not what others tell us we are or ought to be.

The recent conversations I have had with clergymen, both gay and straight, have led me to view the church's hostility toward homosexuality as a manifestation of man's limitations, not God's. I have even found among some clergymen a readiness to welcome and help homosexuals. Recently Father Neale Secor, rector of St. Mary's Episcopal Church in Manhattan, wrote me that his vestry was prepared to help us in any way it could, out of "an awareness of indecent and unnecessary oppression of a large group of God's children," and welcomed homosexuals to his congregation. I had been an atheist for years, partly because I could not see a place for homosexuals in the church; even so, it was a great relief not to be excluded any longer from what was at the very least a former home. More importantly, Father Secor's welcome meant that still-believing homosexuals could worship with heterosexuals as their moral and spiritual equals.

I look upon the church as one of the few possible meeting grounds where homosexuals and heterosexuals together can consider the question of what morality really means and how it applies to the life of the homosexual today. I have come to believe that my sinfulness lies not in my acts of love, but in my selfishness and lack of charity, and the sundry others failings I share with nearly all men and women. I believe that whether a man loves a woman or another man is unimportant and basically not a moral issue but a social one. What *is* important and of abiding moral concern is how fully and generously a person lives his life. This precept seems self-evident to me, but it needs to be tested with others. We must search out and define a morality more compassionate than that which still informs most religious opinion on homosexuals and homosexuality.

Most historians agree that the strong prohibition against homosexuality in our society began with the ancient Hebrews, who viewed homosexuality as "an abomination in the eyes of the Lord." Christianity inherited this attitude from Judaism, and until very recently all branches of Judaism and all Christian sects condemned homosexuality. But this hostility is by no means a universal human attitude, as Wainwright Churchill observes in *Homosexual Behavior Among Males: A Cross-Cultural and Cross-Species Investigation.* "It is clear from the cross-species and cross-cultural data," Churchill concludes, "that our moral judgments and our anxieties in this matter are at considerable variance both with the facts of nature and with the moral judgments of most other non-Judeo-Christian people."*

The Judeo-Christian attitude has had a profound and wide-ranging effect. English common law was based largely on early church law, so that England, followed by all those nations that used its legal system as a model, had for centuries the most severe laws in the world against homosexual acts. (Nations that have based their legal system on the Napoleonic code—which was, of course, not grounded on church law—generally have no such prohibitions, or less stringent ones.) The psychiatric and psychoanalytic professions have been equally influenced by the Judeo-Christian attitude toward homosexuality. Although many early psychoanalysts, including Freud, were atheists, they were nevertheless strongly affected by the religious traditions in which they grew up, particularly in regard to homosexuality, sex roles, and marriage.

All this has been devastating for the individual homosexual, of course. He felt that access to God had been denied him, that all the majestic rites of church and synagogue celebrated events he could never hope to participate in, that his union with a lover would never be blessed, that there would be no priest, preacher, or rabbi to ease the pain of loss for the surviving partner. And certainly a clergyman whose homosexuality became known would probably be forced to leave the ministry.

Until very recently, the church's centuries-long condemnation of homosexual behavior was as universal and unyielding as that of psychiatry. In 1957, the Church of England led the way toward change with its endorsement of the Wolfenden Report. It was also in the late 1950's that

* Wainwright Churchill, *Homosexual Behavior Among Males: A Cross-Cultural and Cross-Species Investigation* (New Jersey: Prentice-Hall, 1967), p. 86.

both Protestant and Catholic churches in the Netherlands initiated study groups on homosexuality and religion, and that a homosexual wedding was celebrated in a Dutch Catholic church. (When Rome requested the immediate removal of the priest who had officiated, the Dutch bishops refused even to discipline him.) In the United States, in the activist aftermath of the Stonewall riots, the church began to divide on the subject of homosexuality. By and large, the gay cause was supported by only those churches, and by no means all of them, that had supported civil rights causes in the past. For example, the United Methodists, my former church and the largest of the Protestant denominations, has failed to pass even a moderate gay-rights endorsement. And in 1972 a Methodist clergyman from Texas was deposed after he announced his homosexuality at a religious conference. In April 1969 the Council for Christian Social Action of the United Church of Christ adopted a statement of support for gay rights; three years later, they ordained an openly gay minister. The Unitarian-Universalist Association is the only other church that has knowingly ordained an openly gay minister. Meanwhile, the only major divinity school to support homosexuals officially and to admit open homosexuals to all of its programs is the Union Theological Seminary in New York. In 1970 the Lutheran Church in America called for the repeal of laws discriminating against homosexuals, and in 1973 the Unitarian-Universalist Association proposed the establishment of an office on gay rights, which was duly set up. Recently the New York and Michigan dioceses of the Episcopal Church have issued strong statements of support for gay civil rights.

Although none of these churches has as yet gone so far as to issue a statement of acceptance on theological grounds, the support they have given has been of crucial importance to gay activists. Their advocacy of antidiscrimination laws undoubtedly carries more weight with legislators than do the appeals and petitions of small gay groups. Furthermore, as part of a larger effort to accommodate homosexuals, many congregations have allowed emerging gay groups to use their churches for meetings and social events. This in itself is a significant change, for it means that today's homosexuals can get together in an atmosphere that is vastly different from that of the gay bars where previous generations of homosexuals were compelled to gather. Meeting in a church allows a whole new set of impulses to come into play—including the impulse to serve others.

But only a minority of churches support the cause of gay civil rights and welcome homosexuals. The great majority—the Roman Catholic Church, most of the more fundamentalist and Pentecostal Protestant sects, and all branches of Judaism—remain hostile. Indeed, the Catholic Archdiocese of New York led a public fight against anti-discrimination legislation when it came up for consideration by the New York City Council in 1974, and the vigorous campaign it waged was widely credited with being the chief cause of the bill's defeat.

Thousands of homosexuals have left these denominations to join the most rapidly growing gay institution, the Metropolitan Community Churches. The Reverend Troy Perry, a former minister in the Pentecostal Church of God of Prophecy, held the first gay church service in Los Angeles in 1968. Since then more than sixty-five member churches have been established, as well as two gay synagogues—Temple Beth Chayim Chadashim in Los Angeles, and Temple Beth Sinchat in New York.

While many homosexuals have left the Catholic Church to join the Metropolitan Community Churches, others have remained to work for change from within. Dignity, founded in Los Angeles in 1969 by Father Pat Nidorf,

OSA, is an association of gay Catholics whose threefold purpose is "to work for the development of [the Church's] sexual theology and for the acceptance of gays as full and equal members of the one Christ, to work for justice and social acceptance through education and legal reform," and to reinforce the sense of dignity of individual gays by helping them to become "more active members of the Church and society."* The American bishops who were notified of the formation of this Catholic organization did not refuse permission either to priests or to Catholic laymen to join it. There are now some thirty chapters of Dignity in as many cities.

In the following pages a gay Catholic priest, who is a member of Dignity, and a gay rabbi will tell how they discovered their homosexuality and how they have resolved or attempted to resolve the apparent conflict between being homosexual and being a servant of God.

Father Ryan, as I shall call him, does not hide his homosexual orientation from his ecclesiastical superiors or from his fellow priests. He is forty-nine years old.

"The realization that I was gay came in high school English class. I was fifteen. We were reading Walt Whitman, and the teacher mentioned that Whitman was homosexual. I didn't know what the word meant, but I suspected, and I remember hurrying home from school that afternoon and looking up the word in the dictionary and thinking to myself, 'So that's what I am!' I didn't know who to turn to. I just lived with it myself.

"At seventeen I came out, in the sense that I had my first lover. We were together for about three months. I was not yet a believing, practicing Christian. I had been raised a Protestant but rejected it. Then guilt began building up, and self-hatred, and finally, at the age of nineteen, I made

* "Constitution," mimeographed (September 1973).

187

my peace with the church and became a Roman Catholic. I determined to be chaste, but my chaste life didn't last very long. One summer I went out to California to do some research, and within a few days I had a lover. Our relationship lasted the whole summer. Again I had great guilt feelings. I remember going to confession one Saturday afternoon. The priest tried very hard to be understanding, but insisted that I leave my lover and go back to sleeping alone at night. I forget whether I told him I would try or whether I said I couldn't give up my lover. In any event, I didn't give him up, and the guilt went on.

"And then I decided that I couldn't live with myself as gay and also with the Catholic Church. I decided that I had seen through the church's whole deceptiveness, all its false claims. But within a couple of years the guilt took over again.

"I had just finished my graduate studies and was teaching in a city where I knew no one, and I suddenly found myself wanting to return to the church. I became a daily communicant and was active in campus Catholic organizations. I tried to find myself a wife, courted a young woman for several months, and then, when the time came to get engaged, I realized that I couldn't go through with it, that marriage wasn't going to solve my loneliness and sense of isolation. It was then that I began considering the priesthood.

"A little over a year later I became a Jesuit. Since I had already spent two years totally abstaining from sexual activity, that aspect of entering the novitiate did not present a sudden change.

"There were twelve years of training—the novitiate, studying philosophy, teaching, studying theology—and during this time I made many close friends. I was sexually attracted to many of the other seminarians—we all lived in a close community—but I thought that I had finally succeeded in becoming asexual. I considered myself no longer homosexual. I really think I had almost succeeded in convincing myself of this. But then I started thinking about what was happening in the church, and in theology after the second Vatican Council, and wondering what the Christian life was all about and what the church should be about and what Christ was all about. I realized that in most of the Bible God is concerned about justice, acceptance of others, and compassion for others. I realized how much of the Catholic tradition, and the Protestant tradition, too, had fallen into the kind of self-righteousness that Christians call Pharisaism. We had become legalistic. And part of this was because of guilt. We all had a strong sense of guilt, especially because of the sexual repression that the traditions—both Jewish and Christian—created. There was sexual repression, and then feelings of guilt about sexual desires and sexual fantasies and daydreams. And along with the guilt there was a need to fall back on a legalistic morality, a series of do's and don't's so clear that by fulfilling it you could have the sense that you stood right with God. It's so easy, if you have a series of do's and don't's, not to worry about the love of God and love of neighbor. You have ready-made answers for all situations, so you can go on fulfilling the laws and failing to accept others, failing in justice, failing in love.

"The first specific problem of sexual morality I found myself faced with was birth control. I had been taught to be very firm with penitents who practiced this abominable sin. My first difficulties came in the confessional, where peoples' lives were at stake. I began to see that contraception was not an intellectual problem with an inevitable conclusion, that there were people in ill health, people who already had too many children, people who had lost their jobs, and that moral theology simply did not speak to life as people had to lead it. This brought me face to face with the traditional sexual morality in the church, and I began to see that the same principles that applied to the morality of contraception applied to the morality of homosexuality.

"About this time, a professor of moral theology at the seminary where I was teaching arranged a colloquium on homosexuality. There were several people from the gay community, including activist leaders who spoke very openly and freely about their gayness, about their concerns, about the oppression they felt from society and especially from the church. They opened my eyes. I had heard about gay lib; I'd seen a few pictures in the newspapers of zaps, and the whole scene seemed bizarre to me. It was another world. But after that colloquium, I realized that these men and women were my people, my gay brothers and sisters, and that I had *not* succeeded in becoming asexual.

"I had already worked out some of the theological and moral implications of being gay, and I knew that what I had to work out now was the emotional side.

"Not too long after this, the New York chapter of Dignity was formed, and I went to the first meeting. This was the second great breakthrough for me. I was very anxious. But after all, we were there for the same reason: We were all gay Catholics who wanted to meet others like us in a setting other than a bar. I realized I was with my own. At Dignity I could be with gay people who had the same sort of emotional and spiritual background that I had. I also got involved with consciousness-raising groups, which helped me to integrate myself into the gay community.

"In June 1973, during Gay Pride Week, I was asked to contribute to a clergy statement on gay rights. I wrote it and lined up a number of clergymen to sign it. This was my first involvement with a political process and the media.

"Next I was asked to be on the board of directors of the National Gay Task Force. The problem was that the Task Force wanted all of its board of directors to be openly gay people, and for me this presented the challenge of whether to come out publicly or not. The members of the board put no pressure on me to come out publicly, and if I had decided I didn't want to, I probably still would have been made a member.

"Although I had been moving in the direction of coming out publicly for many months, I felt that this was one of the momentous decisions of my life—such as my decision to become a priest had been and, before that, my decision to get into academic life. And now the only thing I regret is that I didn't make the decision a long time ago.

"The morning after our press conference, there was an account of the formation of the National Gay Task Force in the New York *Times*. At breakfast I was sitting alone, and the superior of the house came in and said, rather gruffly, 'Did you see this morning's *Times*?' I said, 'Yes.' 'See the article about you?' 'I saw the article in which I was mentioned.' 'What did you think of it?' 'I thought it was all right as an article.' 'Well, there was something in it I didn't like.' 'Oh, what didn't you like?' 'I didn't like the way they described you.' I said, 'What didn't you like about the way they described me?' 'They referred to you as a homosexual activist.' And I said, 'I *am* an activist, and I *am* homosexual.' And the superior, who had not realized all of this, just said 'Ugh,' and walked off without saying another word.

"But many of the priests and many of my students and friends expressed their support and even admiration.

"Eventually a higher superior asked to see me. He said he simply wanted to find out what was going on in my head. I told him that I saw my act of identifying myself with the gay community as part of my Christian duty, and

I tried to explain the great psychological and spiritual harm the church's traditional attitude toward homosexuality has done to gay people. I said that I felt Christians should not only be for liberation, but should also, to the extent they can, actively participate in liberation. The Bishop's Synod of 1971 urged all Catholics to work to end all forms of injustice and oppression.

"My superior felt that the things I believed and said were things a Christian, a Catholic, should be able to believe and say. In Christ there is neither Jew nor Greek, slave nor free man, male nor female. We are all one in Christ. Which means that there has to be a pluralism within the Church, a pluralism in doctrinal matters, a pluralism in moral attitudes and moral understandings. Of course, there still has to be some bond of unity. But the question is: What should be the basis of our unity? In what should all Christians be united? There has to be a dialogue. And a dialogue can take place only if there is openness, that acceptance of others that Jesus was so concerned about. In other words, we have to agree to disagree. This runs contrary to church tradition, which has always striven for a single standard of belief and understanding and activity.

"The majority of Catholics today think that homosexuals are sick and that homosexual activity is sinful. But God is love. And this is what I think too many Christians have forgotten.

"I'm sometimes asked for advice by other gay Catholics. I begin by saying that we must be ourselves, that our religion is certainly not there to keep us from being ourselves. If we are going to be saved, it's our real selves who are going to be saved, not some role we act out. And gayness is not something to be ashamed of. Gay people can exercise their sexuality in very responsible, loving ways, too. I think that what one should always ask about a sexual relationship is whether it is mutually maturing and loving, or whether it is unloving and destructive. There may be other questions that will have to be asked about the relationship, but that I think is the basic one.

"I've told many of my friends that one of the greatest religious experiences I've ever had was marching in the Gay Pride parade in June 1973. There were about twenty of us in the Dignity contingent—marching down Seventh Avenue on a sunny afternoon, putting our arms around one another. There was a spirit of joy, a spirit of being together. The crowds that were watching were not hostile. At a red light we stopped at, some man in the crowd saw me wearing my Roman collar and came out and handed me a can of beer and said, 'Father, you look thirsty.' This is what I consider religion."

The opposition of Jewish religious leaders to homosexuality has been as intractable as that of Catholic leaders. To date, only three rabbis have spoken up for gay civil rights. Though there are several gay rabbis—I have met five myself, and there are many more, as we shall see from the following account—none of them has come out publicly.

"I was born in Russia in 1943 of extremely Orthodox Hassidic parents," says a thirty-one-year-old gay rabbi who now lives in New York City. "Both my father's and my mother's family had been rabbis back to the ninth century. One of my ancestors was considered to have been the greatest rabbi in Eastern Europe since Maimonides; ironically, another wrote all the rules against homosexuality in Eastern Europe in the seventeenth century. We were a very traditional Hassidic family, observing all the commandments, positive and negative, of the Torah.

"There were nine of us in all—but only two of us are still alive. My two older brothers and four of my five sisters died in German concentration camps. My surviving sister married a Catholic, and she was disowned by my mother and father. They actually sat *shiva*, the service for the dead, for her. I was the elder of the two sons born after the war. I was my father's Kaddish, destined to be his successor, the *rebbe* of our sect. But I, too, have been disowned by my parents. My younger brother, who was also gay, committed suicide when he was nineteen.

"When I was seven we moved to Jerusalem, to the ultra-Orthodox section of Mea Sh'arim. Six years later, my parents got divorced. My mother was given custody of my brother and me, though generally in Orthodox Judaism, where the man is the master, it's the father who gets custody of the children.

"Until my parents divorced, my schooling had been entirely in ultra-Orthodox yeshivas. After the divorce I came to live with my sister in America and went to a more or less typical American school. The values of the children at this school really shocked me. Most of them were upper-middle class—the sons and daughters of lawyers, doctors, businessmen—and their interest in going to college was more to get a good job and make a name for themselves than in the value of study for itself, which had been one of the bases of my education.

"When I was sixteen, my father decided that it was time for me to marry. He had been married when he was fifteen or sixteen, and so had my mother. When I was born he had made a *shidach*, a betrothal, for me with the granddaughter of a cousin of his, who was now living in Israel. When he told me that she was to be my wife, I was completely traumatized. She didn't interest me; living in Mea Sh'arim didn't interest me; and getting married didn't interest me at all. I went through about two or three months of quarreling with my father, but I never mentioned the real reason I didn't want to get married: I was gay.

"I first realized that I was gay when I was about eight or nine, and I started having homosexual experiences

194

when I was fourteen. I knew that in Jewish law this was punishable by death. I was supposed to marry, not so much to live with a woman as to provide my parents with grandchildren—someone to continue the family name.

"At one holiday I had noticed a fairly attractive girl who seemed intelligent and rebellious. This appealed to me. I did not want a woman who, like my mother, was just there to serve a tyrant and to take care of the children. I was interested in living with someone who would be more of a peer. The whole family talked it over and finally convinced my father that he should try to arrange a marriage between this girl and me. I was sixteen; she was almost eighteen.

"But after we married I found that our life together was almost an exact duplicate of my parents' life together. My wife's independence very quickly disappeared, her life revolved completely around me, and she abandoned all other interests to take care of the home and wait for children— which I didn't want to have.

"I was married for three years, and the last two were pretty horrible. We divided our time between New York City, where I was going to college, and Israel, where we spent the summer and a week at Passover. I was having gay relationships in both countries.

"My gay friendships gave me what I had hoped to find in my marriage but had not found—someone I could be close to sexually, emotionally, and intellectually. As a result, I became increasingly critical of my wife, increasingly cold and remote. We wanted different things from life, and I did not believe we could create a life together. Finally, we got a divorce.

"After I left my wife, I met a man I loved. This feeling of love for another individual was completely new to me. I had been taught to love God, to love the Jewish community, to love the world; but these more abstract kinds of love didn't affect my practical or personal life. Love was part of my ideology, but it was very difficult to concretize.

Now I was in love with a man. I realized that my love was not something evil but, in fact, was good, both for my lover and for me—even though it conflicted with my entire upbringing.

"I had been raised to think that since God had directly given certain commandments to all Jews for all time, we were morally and spiritually different from and, in fact, superior to, other people. Moreover, having been brought up as the *rebbe*'s son, I believed that I belonged to the moral and spiritual elite of my people. I was not permitted, and was taught not to need, the company of anyone outside my immediate family except those children whose fathers were of the same status as my father. Even in America, I had been socialized into thinking that I shouldn't associate with anyone who came from a lower economic class. But here I was living with a man who was not Jewish, who came from a lower economic class, and whose basic philosophy was one of hedonism, not one of total service to other people.

"Another thing was that because of my father's brand of Hassidism, I had been taught never to express emotion —and not even to express a personal opinion unless it came from an intense analysis of Talmudic texts. Women expressed emotion; men didn't. Women formed intense personal relationships; men studied and observed the law. Women spoke foreign languages; men spoke Yiddish and read Hebrew. Men were superior in every way to women. But here I was, a man who formed intense personal relationships, spoke foreign languages, and was learning to express emotion!

"The central question for me was: How could I reconcile my being a religious Jew with my homosexuality? It was a question I had to deal with totally on my own.

"As I came to grips with my own gayness, I came to see Judaism not as a religion in the American sense but as a life style, as a way of expressing relationship to God by relating to the world through certain forms.

"Obviously, within the Orthodox and Conservative movements, I was a sinner. But since I *knew* that my love for this man did not make me less of a person, I began to break away from the strict branches of Judaism and to investigate the ideas of the *Reform* movement. In Reform Judaism, the Talmud is regarded not as something given to the children of Israel by God, but as the product of a historical process. It is incumbent upon each Jewish community to look constantly at this body of knowledge and see what is relevant, what is good for that time. If something is relevant and it works, you keep it; if it isn't relevant or doesn't work, you don't keep it. If something needs to be added, you use the Talmudic process to arrive at new interpretations.

"The only way I could stay within institutional Judaism would be through the Reform movement. I would have to reinterpret, on the basis of my understanding of the texts, every commandment, every ritual, every tradition to see if it had relevance for me in my situation. And if it did not, then I would have to reinterpret it. I could not, for example, put on phylacteries [ritual objects that an Orthodox Jew puts on for daily prayer] every morning just because it's written that I *should* put them on—that would be meaningless. But if wearing phylacteries could be considered only as part of a prayer service, part of the ritual of worshiping God, I could reinterpret this to mean that I should put aside time to worship and praise God in the morning, and that I should also meditate on my own and consider my relationships with other people each day before entering into them once again. This would really mean something to my generation and to me.

"Again, the law says that I must marry, to set up a Jewish home and have a Jewish family. That no longer had any relevance for me. But to marry in the sense of entering into a relationship in order to become close to another individual, to become aware of myself on a personal level so that I could be aware of myself in relation to the world—that made sense.

"In 1970, while I was finishing up my doctorate in Russian Jewish history, I decided that for my own intellectual and spiritual growth, I would go back to rabbinical school. I chose a Reform movement school in Israel; my father was dying, and I wanted to be there. He died soon after I got there, disappointed in everything I had become.

"I had always maintained two separate lives—one with my gay lovers and friends, and one with my family and the synagogue. In Israel I bought a house and lived with the man who had, years before, been my first lover. After the first three or four months at rabbinical school, I was fairly open. I had wanted the people there to first get to know me as one of them; once I had gained their respect as an individual, I thought, my coming out to them would not make any difference. The individual students I came out to gave me tremendous support. So then I came out to several teachers and even to the dean of the school, and I got a lot of support from them, too. In fact, I held a seminar on homosexuality, a subject they had had no contact with before. The whole atmosphere of the school was very open. During that year, too, I organized a gay students' group at Hebrew University, mainly Americans and British and Australians and South Africans.

"Then I decided to finish rabbinical school in New York. There I organized a study group at the school on being gay and Jewish. Several of the students in my class had studied with me in Israel, and they gave me a lot of support. And the other students I came out to were fine, too. Finally, after months of sitting by while homosexuality and such ideas as women becoming rabbis were put down in class, I came out to the faculty. They were just amazed.

One older man said that I needed to get married, that that would solve everything. Others were not as kind. Some of them still refuse to speak to me. The dean of the school told me that I could not continue there unless I went into extended Freudian psychoanalysis. He would grant me a two-year leave of absense to do that, and if at the end of that time I was totally cured, I would be allowed to come back. I told him that I would not accept a jail sentence for being gay from anyone. That's exactly the way I viewed it: being sentenced to two years of analysis for a 'sickness,' for a 'sin' that I didn't—and don't—believe exists.

"I was thrown out of rabbinical school. Several students I had been closely associated with left at the same time. To finish our training we studied with individual rabbis: There was a custom in nineteenth-century Russia that allowed you to be ordained as a rabbi by three rabbis when they felt you were ready.

"Now I'm working with a congregation as an assistant rabbi—that is, as a bar mitzvah teacher, history teacher, Hebrew teacher, and a teacher in adult education. I have spoken on homosexuality from a theoretical point of view quite a bit in my sermons and in my classes. If one of the children or adults calls someone a queer, I call him a kike. A number of adults indirectly tried to find out if I were gay. I finally asked them to ask me what they wanted to ask me, and when they did I told them. That is the way I've been coming out with the congregation.

"Working with children today, I've found out that they know no more about love than I did at their age. So in some of my courses I try to deal with the question. A few of the kids in my congregation are gay—some of them have come out to me and some haven't—and though I can only express my support of gay people in a theoretical way, this does give them some help. For these kids, having a gay teacher or rabbi as a role model is extremely important."

# CHAPTER ELEVEN

# Psychiatry

On December 15, 1973—thirty years after I learned that as a homosexual I was a "constitutional psychopathic inferior"—I sat in the national headquarters of the American Psychiatric Association in Washington, D.C., listening to its president, Dr. Alfred M. Freedman, announce that the board of trustees had voted that morning to remove homosexuality from its official *Diagnostic and Statistical Manual of Mental Disorders.* "Whereas homosexuality per se implies no impairment of judgment, stability, reliability, or general vocational capabilities," Dr. Freedman read from the board's resolution, "therefore be it resolved that the APA deplores all public and private discrimination against homosexuals in such areas as employment, housing, public accommodations, and licensing, and ... that the APA supports and urges the repeal of all legislation making criminal offenses of sexual acts performed by consenting adults in private."

Since it is doctors who ultimately determine whether people are mentally ill or well, the board's vote made millions of Americans who had been officially ill that morning officially well that afternoon. Never in history had so many people been cured in so little time.

Actually, the APA, in a curious compromise move, officially cured only those of us who accept our homosexuality. Those "who are either bothered by, in conflict with, or wish to change their sexual orientation" could still be diagnosed as ill under a new category called "sexual orientation disturbance." For those of us who believed that the biggest "disturbance" in the life of a homosexual was society's determination that he was less than human, this seemed a strange decision—particularly from a group that had been among the most active to condemn us. The APA press release went on to assure that the "change should in no way interfere with or embarrass those dedicated psychiatrists and psychoanalysts who have devoted themselves to understanding and treating those homosexuals who have been unhappy with their lot." The gay activists who had been invited by the leadership of the APA to come to Washington to hear the outcome of the board's deliberations issued a press release of their own, calling into question the board's motives: "The substitute category . . . has been created to prevent a few psychiatrists who make careers of changing homosexuals from being drummed out of their profession." In any event, the compromise and accommodation that had resulted in the "sexual orientation disturbance" listing were clear enough evidence of the politics involved in the psychiatric profession.

To the gay activists gathered in the APA's national headquarters, the board's decision to remove the stigma of illness from all self-accepting homosexuals was of particular significance, not only because they had played an important part in its making, but also because they could view it in its historical perspective. In the past, three great institutions had joined to label homosexual behavior unacceptable: the law, the church, and the medical profession. The law regarded homosexual activity as criminal, the church as immoral, and the medical profession as perverse, if not psychopathic. Yet both the law and the church had begun to ease their strictures against homosexuals before the 1970's. Only the medical establishment remained unyielding, continuing to label homosexuality as an illness.

The law, of course, still posed problems for the homosexual, but its opposition was not absolute, as was that of the medical profession. For one thing, although it was illegal to engage in homosexual acts, it was not illegal to be homosexual. For another, medical judgments were supposedly based on facts, the result of an irreproachably scientific attempt to reveal truth; the law, a series of conventions drawn up to protect citizens, lacked that aura of holiness and was therefore more accessible to change. In fact, the laws of various nations had never agreed on the subject of homosexuality. The Napoleonic code, for example, which is the basis of law in many European and Latin American nations, did not forbid homosexual activity between consenting adults in private. England had recently repealed its law forbidding such activity, as had eight states in this country. Moreover, throughout most of America the laws banning homosexual acts between consenting adults were seldom enforced (under most circumstances, they were impossible to enforce without violating the citizen's right to privacy). And finally, the passage of civil rights legislation in the 1960's could be construed as a commitment on the part of the law to protect the rights of all minorities, including homosexuals.

Neither was the church monolithic in its opposition. Like the law, it distinguished between being homosexual and engaging in homosexual acts. But for the homosexual who could not lead a celibate life, this distinction was not very helpful. Still, the active homosexual could always hope

202

to find forgiveness in the church, as could other sinners. Moreover, the church was beginning to question the condemnation of homosexuality. The Church of England had supported the reforms called for by the Wolfenden Report, the British parliamentary document of 1957 that led to the abolishment of laws proscribing homosexual acts between consenting adults. And beginning in the 1960's, a number of liberal Protestant denominations in America actively backed the homosexuals' struggle for acceptance. Then, too, a homosexual could deal with the problem of not being accepted by his church by changing denominations or by giving up religion altogether.

Medicine alone of the three institutions had a fixed official opinion on homosexuality—namely, that it was an illness. For gay activists, the medical profession proved a uniquely difficult opponent. There was no precedent for rebelling against oppressive medical opinions, as there was for rebelling against oppressive laws. Labeling homosexuality as an illness could be held to represent not merely an opinion or a consensus, but a scientific judgment. Furthermore, medicine was supposed to be a humane institution, and humane societies always regarded it as a sign of progress when a problem was transferred from a legal to a medical plane (the alcoholic is sick; he should be treated not as a criminal but as a patient). Only homosexuals were excepted from this rule: Their behavior was classified as both sick and criminal.

On the subject of homosexuality, then, law and medicine joined forces. The stamp of illness provided by medicine could be used by legislators to justify the old laws that made homosexual behavior a crime. And, following their leaders, employers could use legal precedent and medical opinion to discriminate against homosexuals with total impunity. The ludicrous uses to which the sickness label has been put are perhaps nowhere more clearly exemplified than in the case of a young New Yorker who applied for a job as a taxi driver in 1972. Asked by the licensing examiner why he had been classified 4-F by his draft board, he explained that he was homosexual. He subsequently received a letter from the taxi commissioner stating that before he could obtain a license he must submit a letter from a "certified" psychiatrist attesting to his fitness to drive a cab and that, once licensed, he would have to be examined by a psychiatrist every six months.

To millions of homosexuals, the social consequences of medicine's sickness label were just as painfully evident. And yet no group had ever challenged the health professions. The gay activists who converged on Washington on December 15, 1973, were the first group of patients in history to insist that they were not sick and to demand that the label be removed.

It had taken the gay activists more than a decade to compel the APA to examine the scientific evidence concerning homosexuality and to recognize the social consequences of its labeling. Dr. Franklin Kameny, who attended the APA's 1973 announcement proceedings, began to press for change in 1961 by helping to found the militant Mattachine Society of Washington. Kameny had been fired from his job as an astronomer with the Army Map Service in 1957, on the grounds that as a homosexual he was a security risk. He had fought his case all the way up to the Supreme Court, writing his own eloquent brief after his lawyer gave up his case as hopeless. When the Supreme Court declined to review his appeal, Kameny was convinced that having done all he could as an individual, he would have to initiate a strong organizational drive for gay civil rights. The nation's few other gay groups contented themselves with inviting outsiders in to be educated about homosexuality and, by and large, accepted the psychiatrists' view of them as sick; the Mattachine Society of Washington (MSW) rejected the prevailing psychiatric opinion and stressed social protest and political activism. In the process of fighting for the repeal of oppressive laws against discrimination in hiring, Kameny learned just how harmful the psychiatric label was. In his words, "It always came down to: 'You're disturbed. You're sick. You're mentally ill.' " In 1965, the MSW became the first gay organization to formally oppose the APA's label.

The Stonewall riots of 1969 led to more militant actions, for the new activists had no doubt that the illness label was as invalid as it was damaging. The annual meetings of the APA became the focal point of militant action. In 1970, gay activists interrupted the proceedings in San Francisco to protest the sickness label. At the 1971 meeting in Washington, D.C., Kameny seized the microphone to explain the social consequences of the sickness label for homosexuals. The activists' message was getting through. A number of psychiatrists, including Dr. Judd Marmor, then vice-president of the APA, had begun to advocate dropping homosexuality from the diagnostic manual. And at the 1972 convention in Dallas, a homosexual psychiatrist was, for the first time, invited to take part in a panel discussion on homosexuality. (He wore a mask, but he was audible, and he was not an outsider, but a member of the APA.) Also, Dr. Richard C. Pillard, a Boston psychiatrist who a short time before had come out as a homosexual to a number of his colleagues (and who was the only homosexual psychiatrist to fight openly for change), was able to persuade the members of the Massachusetts Psychiatric Society to introduce a resolution calling for deletion of the term "homosexuality" from the disease nomenclature. The Massachusetts resolution was duly referred to a committee known as the Task Force on Nomenclature and Statutes— or Nomenclature Task Force, for short—which became the new focal point for gay activist pressure.

In the winter of 1972, Ronald Gold, the forty-two-year-old public relations director of the Gay Activists Alliance, and a number of other militants staged a protest at a behaviorists' convention in New York City. After the protest, one interested listener approached Gold. He was Dr. Robert L. Spitzer, an associate professor of clinical psychiatry at Columbia University, who also happened to be a member of the APA's Nomenclature Task Force. Like most psychiatrists, Spitzer knew very few homosexuals—only those he had met through his practice, fewer than ten. And, like most psychiatrists, he had been slow to realize the social consequences of the APA's sickness label. Gold, whose parents had sent him to psychiatrists in his teens to change his sexual preference, was an eloqent spokesman on this subject. His sexual relationships with both men and women had been brief and guilt-ridden and seemed only to reinforce what he had read and what the psychiatrists had told him—that he was sick and that he would always be unhappy. At twenty he had become a heroin addict, and for five years he was on and off heroin and in and out of jail and hospital. It took him years to recover from being considered, and from considering himself to be, sick.

Through Gold, Spitzer met Charles Silverstein, an openly gay psychologist who was the only mental health worker in the GAA. Silverstein, too, had been hurt by psychiatry. At the age of sixteen, when he told his family doctor about his homosexual urges, the doctor had ushered the boy into a back room, as if to keep his office unpolluted. The doctor referred him to a Brooklyn mental health clinic, where "at a time when I was badly in need of help, I was treated coldly and with disdain." Throughout his training as a psychologist, Silverstein recalls, "certain teachers and students were always cracking jokes about queers." He went through psychoanalysis—"seven very painful and damaging years of it"—to change his sexual preference. Finally, at the age of thirty-one, he gave up on analysis and came out as a homosexual. Determined that other homosexuals in need of help should not suffer such emotional wrenching and humiliation, Silverstein founded the Institute for Human Identity, a New York counseling center that treats homosexual patients without assuming that their homosexuality is an illness in itself.

Spitzer arranged a meeting between Silverstein, a number of other homosexuals, and the members of the Nomenclature Task Force, and he invited Gold to speak at the APA's 1973 convention in Honolulu.

Gold, Silverstein, and the others prepared carefully for the meeting with the Nomenclature Task Force, reviewing the literature on homosexuality. One of the most useful studies had been presented to another mental health group, the American Psychological Association, as far back as 1956, by Dr. Evelyn Hooker, a clinical psychologist. Dr. Hooker had been the first to compare a group of non-patient homosexual men—i.e., homosexuals not undergoing therapy—with a control group of heterosexual men of the same age and professional standing. She had found no more pathology in the homosexuals than in the heterosexuals. The only difference between them lay in their sexual preferences. Dr. Hooker's findings were subsequently confirmed by a number of other studies, and Silverstein had built up a thick file. The overwhelming majority of his evidence was not written by psychiatrists, for the psychiatric profession's findings were largely based on the narrow—and skewed—sample of sick homosexuals. It had taken a biologist, Dr. Alfred Kinsey, working with a team of sociologists and psychologists, to show how common homosexual behavior is. It had taken a clinical psychologist, Dr. Hooker, to show how different the results were when a basic piece of scientific methodology—the use of control groups—was employed. And it had taken other nonpsychiatrists, such as anthropologist Clellan S. Ford and psychologist Frank A. Beach, to establish that homosexual behavior is common among all animal species, and that 64 per cent of non-Western societies treat homosexuality as "normal and socially acceptable" for at least some of the population.* Finally, of course, it had taken activists such as Gold and Silverstein to point out to the psychiatric establishment how much suffering had been caused by the use of a psychiatric label.

In Honolulu in May 1973, Ronald Gold became the first open homosexual to take part in an APA panel discussion. His fellow panelists included Drs. Charles W. Socarides and Irving Bieber, the two leading proponents of the illness theory, and Drs. Judd Marmor, Robert J. Stoller, and Richard Green, all of whom advocated removing the sickness label. Dr. Spitzer, who had set up the panel, acted as moderator. The meeting opened with a series of prepared speeches. Gold's speech, "Stop It, You're Making Me Sick," was not an attack on the psychiatric establishment in general—he acknowledged that the psychotherapy he received at the Menninger Clinic had helped him recover from drug addiction—but rather a bitter indictment of the use of the sickness label. "Your profession of psychiatry," he began, "dedicated to making sick people well, is the cornerstone of a system of oppression that makes people sick." He went on to enumerate some of the social consequences of the sickness label: "In New York City, the telephone company has a policy: If you're gay you're not hired, and if they find out you are, you're fired, no matter how long or how well you've worked."† Again: "The federal government is the worst [discriminator], culminating in the military. I have a choice: I can stay out

---

* Clellan S. Ford and Frank A. Beach, *Patterns of Homosexual Behavior* (New York: Harper & Row, 1951), p. 130.
† The telephone company has since changed its policy.

of the service [by admitting to being homosexual] and risk the chance that my file will be used against me for the rest of my life, or go into the service and face a triple risk—dishonorable discharge, no veteran's rights, and the chance that my file will be used against me for the rest of my life."

Gold then brought his case home to the audience by asking them:

If you were an employer, a landlord, or a judge, would I get a job or an apartment or the custody of a child if you thought I had "wild self-damaging tendencies" and "onslaughts of paranoid ideation" [Dr. Charles Socarides] or "grossly defective peer-group relatedness" and "rage reactions disproportionate to the provocation" [Dr. Irving Bieber]? If you were a legislator, would you vote for my full civil rights—or even let me alone in my bedroom—if you thought that my character was "a mixture of the following elements: masochistic provocation and injustice-collecting; defensive malice; ... refusal to acknowledge accepted standards in nonsexual matters; and general unreliability, of a more or less psychotic nature" [Dr. Edmund Bergler]?

Gold went on to attack the methodology used to arrive at such descriptions of homosexual behavior traits—Socarides, Bieber, and Bergler based their conclusions on studies of sick homosexuals and did not use control groups—and to explain that not only were these descriptions used to justify oppressive laws and discriminatory practices, but that they were also terribly destructive to the homosexual's view of himself; in fact, they were themselves a cause of mental disturbance. He concluded by asking his audience to "take the damning label of sickness away from us" and to let the world know they had done so. As a public relations man, Gold was acutely aware that for years the only psychiatric voices that the public had heard on the subject —"the people the media always call on when they want

209

something 'official' about the fags and dykes"—were those of the proponents of the sickness label. It was high time, he felt, that other voices began to be heard.

Encouraged by the reception accorded Gold's speech and the speeches of the other panelists in favor of removing the sickness label, Dr. Spitzer went on to draw up the resolution that the APA's board of trustees voted to accept in December 1973.

Those of us homosexuals who had worked for that resolution had widely different views on psychiatry as it related to us. Charles Silverstein believed that psychotherapy could be effective, provided that the therapist did not regard homosexuality as an illness. Dr. Bruce Voeller was more critical; he felt that his early contact with a psychiatrist who had assured him that he could not possibly be homosexual had doomed him to ten years of sexual confusion and emotional anguish and had led him into an unhappy marriage. As a research biologist, he also believed that psychotherapy was pseudoscientific in that very few of its assumptions had been subjected to systematic study. We had all been struck by how little the psychiatrists who had characterized us as sick knew about homosexuals and the lives we led. After I came out publicly, I made a point of talking to a number of psychiatrists about homosexuality. Few of them, I discovered, knew much, if anything, about long-term relationships, and few had any idea of the number of successful gay physicians and psychiatrists. At the APA's 1973 convention, for example, sixty gay psychiatrists held a secret party on the night of the annual dance. When gay activists informed APA officers of the size of the turnout, the officers were astonished. And yet the sixty gay psychiatrists who showed up for this party represented only a comparatively bold minority of the association's total gay membership.

It is difficult to forgive the psychiatric profession's

naïveté about us, for its consequences have been far-reaching and painful. My own punishing experience with it demonstrates just how much damage it can do.

I had my first contact with a psychiatrist in 1942, when I anxiously told the head of the psychiatry department at Western Reserve Medical School of my homosexual urges and was reassured that I could not possibly be homosexual because "homosexuals don't become doctors, they become hairdressers." (Incredibly, this myth was still intact among health professionals thirty-one years later. In 1973 I was asked to address a combined meeting of the New Jersey Medical Psychiatric Association and the New Jersey Medical Society so that their members could see that "homosexuals aren't all hairdressers; they can be physicians.") In 1943, while I was serving as a medical corpsman in an Army hospital in Cambridge, Ohio, I studied the Medical Corps' official list of diagnoses to find out what I could about homosexuality. I learned that if I turned out to be homosexual I would be classified among the "constitutional psychopathic inferiors." I was not sure precisely what this meant, but I was able to grasp its general import—homosexuals were mentally ill. In 1944, released from the Army to enter medical school, I looked up the Surgeon General's classification of constitutional psychopathic inferiors in my psychiatric textbook and learned that as a homosexual I could be expected to demonstrate the following traits: "lack of appreciation and understanding of the consequences of their acts, inability to form mature judgments and profit by past experience, a general impulsiveness and inability to postpone carrying out certain wishes, a general undependability, and a lack of consideration for the ordinary moral concepts and standards of the group in which they live."* I then looked into Krafft-Ebing's *Psychopathia*

* Edward A. Strecker, Franklin G. Ebaugh, and Jack B. Ewalt, *Practical Clinical Psychiatry* (Philadelphia: The Blakiston Co., 1947), p. 304.

211

*Sexualis*, to discover that homosexuals could look forward to "nothing more or less than a hopeless existence, a life without love, an undignified comedy before human society," and one in which, moreover, "an eventual loss of social position, civic honor, and liberty are involved."* I was young and as doubtful of myself as I was respectful of authority, and it did not occur to me to question the validity of these shattering judgments. It never occurred to me, for example, to check to see what research techniques the authors had used. The cumulative impact of all this was devastating. If I were sexually what my impulses told me I was, I was not only mentally ill and morally stunted, I was also doomed to lead a travesty of a life, a life that would get worse, not better, and that would inevitably end in shame and disgrace.

I have already recounted my meeting with the new head of Western Reserve's psychiatry department, who told me that I should give up medical school for analysis—advice I could not follow, since it was only by becoming a doctor that I could ever earn enough money to pay for analysis. I have already described those four, purgatorial years of waiting to be redefined as a man; they were the most painful part of my entire term as an officially sick man. I should add that they were also economically distressing. I saw my analyst four times a week, at $20 an hour, forty-eight weeks a year for four years—which comes to about $15,000. I had to work incessantly to pay for the analysis, on which I spent more money than on all my living expenses combined.

My analyst, whom I'll call Dr. Snell, was considered to be one of the best psychoanalysts in the Midwest. He was in his early forties, of medium height; he had a paunch and a balding head, and he was absolutely humorless. He was an orthodox Freudian analyst—which meant, among other

* R. Krafft-Ebing, *Psychopathia Sexualis* (New York: Physicians and Surgeons Book Co., 1931), p. 460.

212

things, that he considered homosexuality to be a developmental stage that "normally" preceded heterosexuality. (Orthodox Freudians were often more dogmatic than Freud himself.) Dr. Snell sat, generally silent, while I stretched out on his couch and recalled my past and told him my dreams and freely associated and regressed, recapitulating time and again the anal and oral stages of my development. Several times Dr. Snell broke his silence to say that he was pleased with the way my analysis was progressing. He declared that my heterosexual side was bound to emerge, sooner or later.

I longed for this side of me to appear—in the symbolic language of dreams, which only Dr. Snell could decode; in my responses to the whores I made myself visit or to the two women who did their best to arouse me. In the four years of analysis I did not have a single heterosexual dream; and none of the women I tried to sleep with excited me at all. And yet, the fear of being castrated by women, which Dr. Snell assured me underlay my homosexuality, never emerged either. Meanwhile, Dr. Snell made it clear to me that I must not "act out" my neurosis by having homosexual experiences; he warned me that if I did so, he might terminate my analysis. I could not completely give up homosexual relationships, but the few I had during those dully miserable years were utterly devoid of affection and left me feeling tremendously guilty.

Cut off from women, striving to detach myself from men, doubting that I could even be close friends with anyone, I felt robbed of all sense of identity. I was probably a less alert, compassionate, and skillful physician than I should have been. My mind was preoccupied with guilt, with dreams, with forlorn hopes, and with a sense of inadequacy that my sessions with Dr. Snell drove home four times a week.

The few insights I gained during analysis were nothing

compared to its overriding message—that I was inherently impaired because of my sexual orientation and that if I could not change it, I was doubly a failure. I left analysis convinced that I had no talents. I would be a physician, yes, but a mediocre one. I had no sense that I could be a professor, much less a health services administrator in a large city.

I now believe myself to be a capable person in many areas, but I wasted years before accepting it. What makes this even more infuriating now is that the sense of inadequacy that crippled me was not necessarily linked with my homosexuality—a distinction my analyst failed to observe or, at any rate, failed to impart to me. I had a number of personality problems apart from those arising from my sexual identity, but these were never treated. I also had problems with my sex life, just as many heterosexuals do, but these, too, remained unmentioned and untreated. Dr. Snell convinced me that I could not love—indeed, that no homosexual could love. Dr. Snell had thoroughly indoctrinated me to believe that my love for men was a clear symptom of neurosis. And it was easy to find neurotic symptoms, both in myself and in my gay friends, to substantiate this point of view. I was not aware that psychiatrists' interpretations of what constitutes a neurotic symptom differ. I was not even aware of how common neurotic symptoms are in the population at large: The most comprehensive studies estimate that more than 50 per cent of the population at any time exhibit some psychiatric symptoms.*

This conviction that homosexuals were all emotionally impaired made learning to live a gay life exceedingly difficult when I moved to New York. I was hyperconscious and painfully oversensitive; the tiniest slip (a letter I

* Mervyn Susser, *Community Psychiatry: Epidemiologic and Social Themes* (New York: Random House, 1968), pp. 214–15.

forgot to mail, an appointment for which my lover was late) meant that we were doomed. Everything my acquaintances or I did was a sign of some psychiatrically unsound quality. I could not accept any of my own or others' behavior at face value. Naturally, with this tension and suspicion always in the background, my relationships were not the happiest or most successful. And, of course, their failure gave further proof that Dr. Snell and the establishment he represented were right.

It took me almost twenty years to recover from the effects of my analysis—which is to say, it took me almost twenty years to regard myself and other homosexuals as worthwhile and capable.

One obvious conclusion to be drawn from my story is that homosexuals must select their psychiatrists with even greater care than other patients. The outcome of psychotherapy always largely depends on the competence and approach of the psychiatrist, but homosexuals must be particularly careful, since the psychiatrist who regards homosexuality as an illness will obviously have a different approach to homosexual patients from that of one who does not. And, regardless of that APA resolution, many psychiatrists cling to that belief. A dissident group at the December 1973 meeting demanded a referendum on removing the sickness label; 36 per cent of the doctors who voted on it thought the label should stick. Moreover, many of those who persist in this belief are, I think, apt to have developed a form of mental illness themselves, a sort of "unconscious homophobia." Perhaps threatened by the unhappy or disturbed homosexuals on whom they have based their judgment of the rest of us, they are convinced that any means are justified to "cure" the patient of his love of men. Psychiatrists who make use of aversion therapy (in which the patient is shown films of homosexuals making love and then given a pill that induces

·

215

vomiting) may be suspected of suffering from this ailment. After all, they watch the movies, too.

But even assuming that the majority of psychiatrists are willing to uphold the new resolution, there is still much doubt about how effective they can be. The new diagnosis, "sexual orientation disturbance," makes it possible for psychiatrists to hold out the hope to troubled homosexuals (and to the troubled parents of homosexuals) that extended psychotherapy can alter preference. But can it?

Many psychiatrists claim that they can alter sexual preferences; many others say it is impossible. Dr. Judd Marmor, who has talked to a large number of psychiatrists about this subject and is familiar with the cases reported in the professional literature, told me that those who believe they can effect a change claim success with about a third of the patients they treat. Such claims, however, are not based on solid evidence.

One psychiatrist who claims to be able to change sexual preference is remarkably vague about the outcome of his therapy in the cases he describes. I know a man who came out of four years of therapy with him with no heterosexual desires, yet in the final week of analysis the doctor advised him to visit a prostitute at least once a week. Another psychiatrist I know reported that a patient of his had begun to visit a prostitute, but had then announced that he could not afford to pay both his analyst and the prostitute and that he preferred to have the services of the prostitute. This was accepted as proof that the patient was cured.

Such instances point up a major weakness of modern psychiatry and psychology: The knowledge upon which they are based is not yet scientific. The trial-and-error process of research is still at a very primitive stage, and it is likely to be slow in developing. There are several reasons for this. Psychiatric symptoms are nowhere near as concrete as physical ones, which makes them harder to isolate and describe. A lot of psychiatric research has to be based on patients' own accounts of their histories, experiences, and feelings, and these renditions are far from absolutely reliable. Furthermore, the researchers who assemble these data and draw conclusions from them may well introduce their own bias as they do so: In so ill-defined and vague an area, personal prejudice is almost impossible to eliminate. The result is that the causes of most emotional illnesses remain unknown. Indeed, debate still continues about whether psychiatric labels identify true illness or are merely social judgments.

And if the question of how to define mental illness is not easily resolved, the effect of treatment is even harder to evaluate. A recent study by Saghir and Robins* found that many homosexuals who had undergone psychotherapy "felt negative" about their experience, believing either that it had not helped them or that it had left them in worse shape than before.

Not only do psychotherapists claim questionable cures while failing to report adverse effects of therapy, they also fail to define precisely what they mean by a change in sexual preference. Does it mean that the formerly exclusively homosexual patient is now having occasional heterosexual experience while continuing to have homosexual urges and fantasies? Does it mean that he is able to marry and have children? Does it mean that he has given up sex altogether? Until a definition is offered and generally accepted, claims of cure are virtually meaningless.

Saghir and Robins conclude: "The simple fact is that there is no reliable replicated method offering a cure to randomly selected groups of homosexuals. . . . Those who have written about a cure for homosexuality have been largely unable to detail the specifics involved, the methods

* Dr. Marcel T. Saghir and Dr. Eli Robins, *Male and Female Homosexuality* (Baltimore: Williams & Wilkins, 1973), p. 112.

to be followed in order to effect a cure, and the criteria for cure itself.*

At present, then, the question of whether psychotherapy can or cannot alter sexual preference remains unresolved, except in the minds of those who are allowing themselves to be convinced by spurious evidence.

It is my firm belief, given all this confusion and the absence of proved satisfactory results from psychotherapy, that a homosexual troubled by his homosexuality should seek help first from a gay activist group or a gay counseling center. One major cause of the homosexual's disturbance is that he does not know anything about homosexuality; he needs information. There is no body of scientific knowledge about homosexuality (and psychiatrists may not be the first to be aware of it when and if there is); we are only beginning to understand what a healthy life is for a gay person. The nonprofessionals who work with homosexuals and cope with their problems every day may be the best informed. Most large cities have such centers. They are staffed by psychiatrists, psychologists, social workers, and nonprofessional peer counselors, most of whom are homosexual themselves.

Another benefit these centers offer is to introduce young homosexuals to gay men who are happy and who can therefore provide moral support and a sense of community. Two Kinsey Institute sociologists, Martin S. Weinberg and Colin J. Williams, explained it as follows:

Learning from other homosexuals who function as role models seems to be one major process [in learning to adjust to one's homosexuality]. In addition, from other homosexuals one learns more about subtle stereotypes of heterosexuals, how to handle a homosexual social identity and so on. At the same time, other homosexuals give one support in the trial and error process of becoming homosexual. Acculturation to a

* Saghir and Robins, p. 318.

homosexual way of life routinizes behaviors that perhaps initially seemed shameful; this makes acceptance of the self-label of "homosexual" easier.... In general, our findings appear to support the notion, suggested by the societal reaction approach, that associating with similarly situated others enhances a sense of well-being.*

Many parents are afraid that such organizations tend to push people in doubt about their sexual identity into homosexuality. This is most emphatically untrue. Even if gay activists wanted to influence the people coming to them for guidance (which they do not), is it rational to fear that although heterosexual psychiatrists, with the full weight of society's approval backing them up, have failed to alter sexual preferences for most of their patients, activist leaders will succeed in the other direction? Sexual preferences are established very early in life—certainly before the age of five or six. These groups merely help clarify the issues for confused people—a process that, interestingly, has led some young men to the realization that they are after all heterosexual—and offer some hope to those who thought that their homosexuality condemned them to a life of failure and unfulfillment. The organizations are a grass-roots solution to a problem that the psychiatric establishment has not even begun to face.

It would have been better for us if psychiatrists had ignored homosexuality altogether, but they have not. Instead, they have actively used their position of power and respect to make our lives more difficult. That this was done, in many cases, with the best of intentions does not lessen the damage it has caused.

Even the December 1973 resolution has its harmful effects. By maintaining a "sexual orientation disturbance"

* Martin S. Weinberg and Colin J. Williams, *Male Homosexuals* (New York: Oxford University Press, 1974), p. 271.

category, the APA has held out a hope (largely unjustified, as we have seen) that therapy can change sexual preference. One consequence of this is that many thoughtful people are led to regard the gay civil rights struggle as a matter of no great urgency, since all homosexuals have to do to be treated as first-class citizens is to undergo extended psychotherapy. A second consequence is that parents— and perhaps even employers—can continue to insist that the homosexuals in their charge undergo psychoanalysis. As a result, the majority will continue to be regarded as failures by their parents or fired by their employers. Moreover, not only does the very expensive process of therapy frequently fail to effect a cure, it also frequently has adverse effects. If the psychiatric establishment genuinely cared about the mental health of homosexuals, its members would recommend that they seek help where it is available at little or no cost—namely, at gay counseling centers.

Psychiatrists and psychoanalysts have published books and papers about homosexuality that, apart from being scientifically invalid, have been socially irresponsible, causing mental torment to hundreds of thousands, if not millions. For years, practically the only descriptions of homosexuals that could be found were those in psychiatric texts, descriptions abstracted from the case histories of a few sick individuals. As Dr. Wardell Pomeroy has observed: "If my concept of homosexuality were developed from my practice, I would probably concur in thinking of it as an illness. I have seen no homosexual man or woman in that practice who was not troubled, emotionally upset, or neurotic. On the other hand, if my concept of marriage in the United States were based on my practice, I would have to conclude that marriages were all fraught with strife and conflict, and that heterosexuality is an illness."*

* "Homosexuality," in *The Same Sex: An Appraisal of Homosexuality*, Ralph W. Weltge, ed. (Philadelphia/Boston: Pilgrim Press, 1969), p. 13.

Psychiatrists and psychoanalysts, posing as experts on all homosexuals instead of only on the disturbed ones who wandered into their offices, have allowed their testimony to be used to retain antihomosexual laws and to prevent the passage of legislation forbidding discrimination against homosexuals—laws that affect great numbers of people. At the APA's 1973 convention, Dr. Judd Marmor said: "I have only within the past year seen a highly intelligent and capable government employee of almost twenty years of service, with an impeccable record, fired from his job when his private and discreet homosexual life was discovered. To bolster its case, the government used Socarides' testimony that this man, simply because he was homosexual, had to be a seriously disturbed and unstable person, regardless of his excellent work adjustment and record." Did the APA repudiate Dr. Socarides' testimony or take any sanctions against him? It did not. It did nothing.

The APA's removal of the sickness label may lead in time to our being accorded the same respect and given the same right to live and work in society as others. In the meantime, perhaps the best way for organized psychiatry and individual psychiatrists to help the nation's homosexual population is to refrain from speaking publicly as if they were scientific authorities on the subject. In the past their eloquence has had disastrous consequences. Now their silence might be therapeutic.

CHAPTER TWELVE

# The Law

Back in the 1950's, on nights when I set out for one or another of New York's dingy gay bars, I often felt part of a criminal class—a class that included drug addicts, prostitutes, and the Mafia men who owned the gay bars in those days. During the day I never had this sense of being a criminal. My colleagues at the office regarded me as straight; society in general regarded me as eminently respectable—I was, after all, a member of the medical establishment. And I certainly had no reason to fear the police—at least until nightfall. To be homosexual is not against the law, but throughout most of the United States most ways of seeking out homosexual partners and all ways of making homosexual love are, so that whenever I made love I was engaging in a criminal activity.

On those nights when I went in search of love, I almost invariably wound up descending into a world peopled by criminals and controlled by criminals. Because gay bars catered to men helpless not to engage in unlawful acts, they were owned and operated by men who specialized in making crime pay, and they were subject to police raids.

I never met any of the members of organized crime who owned these bars, but occasionally some dark, heavy, taciturn man would be pointed out to me as a syndicate boss. Often a similarly foreboding bouncer was posted at the door to turn heterosexual couples away. The atmosphere was reminiscent of a speakeasy in Prohibition days, but not so merry as speakeasies are said to have been.

Whenever policemen entered, I eyed them with fear—until I learned that generally they came in only to be paid off. Actually witnessing these payoffs strengthened my feeling of belonging, if only peripherally, to the big-city underworld. I was never caught in a police raid on a gay bar, but many of the bars I had visited from time to time were raided and closed down. Often, just before a mayoralty election, there would be a concerted period of raids; in 1962, for example, Mayor Wagner's police closed almost every gay bar in the city. (In New York City, bars are no longer raided merely because they are gay bars, and the Mafia no longer exercises complete control over them —some are owned by gay men who have no connection with the underworld—but in most cities gay bars are still owned and operated by criminals.)

In the hierarchy of criminals, I thought the police would probably consider me somewhere between a prostitute and a drug addict. I doubted that I could count on them to protect me if they knew I was homosexual. This left me feeling completely at the mercy of real criminals.

One Sunday afternoon in 1965, shortly after I had broken up with Steve, my vulnerability to criminal acts was brought home to me very forcefully. I was walking down Third Avenue, on Manhattan's East Side, not consciously cruising, but in the back of my mind hoping that I would meet someone. I had always been very wary of cruising. The risks were too high: The man I picked up might rob or attack me once we got to my apartment or his, or he might be a plainclothesman. (In those pre-Lindsay days, such entrapment was still a realistic expectation.) I had been walking for about ten minutes when a man of about twenty-five began to look me over. After the initial eye contact of cruising, one goes through various rituals trying to make sure that the person really is gay and sizing him up for safety. A common first step is to pause in front of a store window and look in; if the other man pauses and looks in, too, one can start talking about something in the display. Then, if everything seems all right, the bolder of the two will ask the other to come to his place for a drink.

That afternoon I was feeling too cautious even to stop at a store window. But I did walk noticeably slower. So did the young man. At the corner, while we were waiting for a traffic light to change, he began to talk to me. We walked for a long time together, perhaps an hour, talking. He told me that he was a printer and described in some detail his work in the union, which made me feel that he was safe. On the other hand, he did not strongly attract me, and I did not feel that he was very attracted to me, either. But he walked me to the door of my apartment house where, more out of politeness than desire, I asked him if he wanted to come up and have a drink.

As we entered the lobby, the doorman said, "Hello, Doctor." This made me a little nervous, since I had naturally not told the young man who I was.

Up in my apartment, he said, "You've got a nice place here. I wish I had one like it." I remember saying something like, "You probably will one day." "No, I won't," he said, rolling up his sleeve to show me the needle marks.

For a second I didn't understand what he wanted, and I said, "Oh, that's too bad." The next moment he was holding a knife to me and saying that he was desperate, that he had to have a fix. I told him I didn't have any drugs in my apartment. He forced me to open all the drawers and closets. Then he demanded all my money and my watch. I gave him what I had on me—only about ten dollars (when going to the bars or out to cruise, gay men generally take only small sums of money)—and my watch, which, along with some odds and ends, he stuffed into his pockets.

Then, getting ready to leave, he said, "Don't call for help or have me stopped downstairs, because if you do I'll tell them you're a queer. And if you report me to the cops, I'll tell *them* you're nothing but a fucking queer."

He had known all along that the knife he carried was not his most dangerous weapon to me, that I would give him all the money I had in the world just to keep him from shouting those words. How could I ask the doorman to stop him when all he would have to say to ruin me is that I had invited him up to have sex with him? And how could I tell the police when I myself was a criminal in their eyes?*

I have never been arrested, but as I said, whenever I make love, I am engaging in an activity that is considered criminal in New York State. Indeed, homosexual activities are considered criminal in all but the following American states—Colorado, Connecticut, Delaware, Hawaii, Illinois, North Dakota, Oregon, California, New Mexico, Maine, Washington, and Ohio—and the District of Columbia, each of which has adopted the 1955 model penal code of the American Law Institute, which holds that homosexual acts between consenting adults are legal. The United States, with the aforementioned exceptions, and the Soviet Union are the only great nations in the world that still

---

* In *Male and Female Homosexuality* (pages 163 and 165), Saghir and Robins found that 37 per cent of homosexuals had been robbed, physically assaulted, threatened, or blackmailed at least once and that 57 per cent of these had, like me, not reported these offenses to the police.

outlaw consensual homosexual acts between adults. The Napoleonic code, which forms the basis of law in France and in most of the Latin countries, does not outlaw such acts.

Because most homosexual acts take place in private, very few homosexuals are arrested under the so-called sodomy laws, which specifically outlaw certain sexual acts and which remain on the law books in forty-seven states. Many, however, are arrested for having sex in public places such as parks (more specifically, as Marilyn Haft, a lawyer for the American Civil Liberties Union, pointed out in a speech delivered at the 1974 meeting of the American Bar Association, in "some secluded area in which heterosexual activity would hardly be penalized"). In North Dakota—which allows consensual homosexual acts between adults in private —the sentence for a first conviction on the charge of committing a homosexual act in a public place is seven to ten years in prison, and in Arkansas, which makes all homosexual acts illegal, it can be as much as twenty years.

The great majority of arrests do not occur as a result of homosexual acts committed either in private or in public places but as a result of the homosexual's search for friends and partners. In making these arrests, the police can invoke a variety of laws: engaging in disorderly conduct, loitering to solicit for deviate sexual purposes, and even vagrancy. Repealing the sodomy laws alone, then, will not stop police harassment. A homosexual still runs a greater risk of being arrested in any large city in Illinois, which has repealed its sodomy laws, than in New York City, which has not. It is not the laws themselves that count so much as the sophistication and tolerance of the individual policeman.

It is impossible to obtain reliable data as to the percentage of America's homosexual population that has been arrested. Two recent studies, both based on a sampling of men who belong to homophile organizations, have come up with different figures: one found that 25 per cent—the other that 37 per cent—had been arrested for some activity connected with homosexuality. Both figures seem exceedingly high to me and to my gay friends, most of whom would set the figure at about one per cent. I can only suppose that a disproportionate number of men who had been arrested joined homophile groups in the late 1950's and the 1960's in order to establish ties with the gay community and to work to change existing legislation.

Arrest, even when it does not result in conviction, is, needless to say, one of the most terrifying things that can happen to a homosexual. His reputation, his career, often enough his whole life, are at stake.

One of my friends, now a highly regarded New York City obstetrician, was arrested in 1955 for having sex with another man in a secluded area of a city park. (He was then an interne living in a hospital and could not bring a man to his room.) He called me in desperation. There was no time to discuss how foolish he had been; there was barely time to save his career, which now stood in the gravest jeopardy. If word were to get out about his appearance in court, he would doubtless be expelled from his interne-ship program. But keeping his case out of the newspapers was a minor problem compared to the one posed by possible conviction: He could very well lose his license to practice medicine in the state of New York.

I called the most successful homosexual lawyer I knew. I did not hold out much hope for his being able to help out. For one thing, he specialized in corporate law. For another, homosexual lawyers did not then handle cases involving homosexuals for fear that this would lead their colleagues to suspect them. Up until 1973, when the New York Court of Appeals ordered that a self-proclaimed homosexual be admitted to the bar, no known homosexual had ever been admitted, and any lawyer convicted of engaging in a homosexual act could expect to be automatically disbarred.

To my surprise and relief, the lawyer said that he would do what he could. He explained that the only way to save my physician friend's reputation was to keep the case from coming to court, and that the only way to do this was to pay someone off. He himself never resorted to this practice, but he could put me in touch with lawyers who did. These lawyers were themselves straight, he added, and had built up their practices serving homosexual clients who would pay a great deal to avoid the publicity of a court hearing. He called one of these lawyers. My friend and I waited anxiously for five days; then word came back that $3,000 would keep the case out of court. Internes were not paid much in those days, and my friend could hardly ask his parents for such a sum without explaining why he needed it. So a number of our gay friends pooled their resources, and he was saved.

I have more than once perjured myself to keep homosexual friends from being convicted of having committed homosexual acts in public. In all the other areas of my life I have always been scrupulously honest. But refusing to lie to spare a gay person years in prison or the possible loss of his livelihood seemed to me a strange sort of morality. My own life was a lie so long as I tried to pass as straight; indeed, I was compelled to lie every day to protect my secret.

One person I perjured myself for was a twenty-eight-year-old man who had been arrested for committing a homosexual act late at night in a New York City park. Conviction in his case, too, would have meant utter ruin. Eight years before, he had been sentenced to two years in a penitentiary for passing bad checks. This had been at a time when he was having great difficulty accepting his homosexuality, but since then his behavior had been exemplary. He now had a good job to which he had just been promoted. I liked him; I believed him to be a basically decent and valuable person. It did not seem right that he should be destroyed for engaging in acts that I, too, engaged in, although more circumspectly.

And so I lied. I went to court on his behalf, testifying as his personal physician, which I had become the moment he asked me for help. I was then medical director of the Gouverneur Health Services Program, associate director of Beth Israel Hospital, and a Fellow of the New York Academy of Medicine. My friend's lawyer asked me in court if the defendant were homosexual and if he would engage in homosexual acts. I answered very firmly that he was not and that he would not. The judge asked me if I was certain, and I said yes. He then asked me if I was aware of the defendant's previous conviction. I said I was. The case was dismissed. Now, some ten years later, this man is living with another man in a stable long-term relationship, and he is still employed by the same company.

It is easy to be critical of gay men who commit homosexual acts or solicit partners in public places. But it must be understood that for the most part those who resort to such things have been deprived of any other way of meeting gay men. None of the gay men I know of who have established long-term relationships and a community of friends have been arrested under such circumstances. And fortunately, Mayor Lindsay's ban on police entrapment has reduced the number of such arrests from more than 100 each week (in 1966) to "virtually none."*

It is easy to forget that homosexuals do nothing in bed that is not also done by many heterosexuals. This is something that is obscured by the terminology of many laws. In keeping with society's attitude toward homosexual acts

* Arno Karlen, *Sexuality and Homosexuality: A New View* (New York: W. W. Norton, 1971), p. 610.

229

as crimes too heinous to be mentioned, sex statutes contain such phrases as "carnal copulation" (is not all copulation carnal?), "the abominable and detestable crime against nature," and "any unnatural, lascivious act." Clearly, then, these laws, by avoiding any specific mention of homosexuality, apply to heterosexuals as well. Yet they are generally enforced only in the case of homosexuals.

The law has had the same kind of wide and sorry effect on the nation's homosexual population as has psychiatry. Both institutions have wreaked havoc in the lives of numerous individual homosexuals, of course, but their harmfulness has by no means stopped there. Radiating out from those individual cases is a message—homosexuals are on the one hand criminals and on the other incurably tainted by illness—that has been read, believed, and acted on by homosexuals and heterosexuals alike. Thus the principal victims of the law and its unjust—and unjustifiable—assumptions are not the handful of homosexuals who are tried and convicted, but the millions of others who have not been and probably never will be arrested.

The law has been used, most notably at all levels of government, to justify denying employment to known homosexuals. It was only in 1974 that the U.S. Civil Service Commission revised its policy of regarding homosexuality as a bar to employment.

Bonding companies continue to refuse to bond and insurance companies continue to refuse to insure known homosexuals because of their criminal status.

Homosexual organizations have been refused the right to incorporate themselves. For example, in 1972, the Secretary of State of New York refused the Gay Activists Alliance permission to incorporate, explaining that homosexual acts were "illegal" and "contrary to public policy." This decision was successfully challenged, however.

A number of gay activist groups have been denied tax-exempt status by the Internal Revenue Service on the grounds that it was not in the best interests of the community to encourage their existence. These decisions are being challenged in the courts.

The Immigration and Naturalization Service excludes and deports homosexual aliens under Sections 1182 and 1251 of Title 8 of the U.S. Code, which permit the exclusion of those "afflicted with psychopathic personality, or sexual deviation, or mental defect." In June 1974 Dr. John W. Spiegal, president of the American Psychiatric Association, wrote a letter to the commissioner of the service pointing out that homosexuality was no longer classified as an illness. Together with the executive director of the American Civil Liberties Union and the heads of a number of gay civil rights and education and legal aid organizations,* Dr. Spiegal requested the service to exercise its discretionary power to halt its actions against homosexuals.

The reply these petitioners received from Acting General Counsel Sam Bernsen, dated August 8, 1974, is a document of considerable interest, revealing how psychiatry, religion, and law interact and interlock to discriminate against homosexuals. The following three excerpts show the gradual disintegration of a defense that begins with a psychiatric finding, since discredited by the psychiatrists themselves.

The Manual for Medical Examination of Aliens issued by the Public Health Service of the Department of Health, Education and Welfare states in chapter 6, page 5, that a person who is diagnosed as a sexual deviate comes within the legal term

* The Lambda Legal Defense and Educational Fund was established in 1973 by six young attorneys, some of whom are openly homosexual, to initiate or join in legal actions that involve decisions affecting large numbers of homosexuals and to provide legal advice to the homosexual community. There has been a desperate need for this, since probably fewer than ten homosexual lawyers have come out publicly.

"psychopathic personality," which is equivalent to the medical designation "personality disorder."

In short, the rationale for barring foreign homosexuals from entering the country and for deporting them is that they suffer from a personality disorder. Mr. Bernsen adds:

The United States Supreme Court in *Boutilier* v. *INS*, 387 U.S. 118 (1967) stated its conclusion that the Congress used the phrase "psychopathic personality" not in the clinical sense but to effectuate its purpose to exclude from entry all homosexuals and other sexual perverts. The Supreme Court upheld the Service position that an alien is deportable if he was excludable under Section 212 (a) (4) of the Immigration and Nationality Act on the ground that he was a homosexual at the time of entry.

In other words, foreign homosexuals are not barred or deported because they suffer from a personality disorder but simply because they are homosexuals. Having thus moved himself back to square one, Mr. Bernsen starts all over again, switching to the safer (because vaguer) grounds of morality.

Naturalization, as you undoubtedly know, is a judicial function. However, the Service position is that a petitioner for naturalization who is or has been a homosexual during the relevant statutory period is precluded from establishing the good moral character required for admission to citizenship. See Petition of Olga Schmidt, 289 N.Y. Supp. 2d 89 (1968). Although some courts have admitted homosexuals to citizenship, *In re Labady*, 326 F. Supp. 924 (1971), this Service will continue to recommend to the courts that homosexuals be denied citizenship on the ground that they do not possess the good moral character required for citizenship.

As I write this, I can look up from my desk at two documents bearing the seal of the Mayor of New York. One proclaims Mayor Lindsay's appointment of me as administrator of the Health Service Administration, the other as Commissioner of Health. Both contain these words: "Know ye, that reposing special trust and confidence in the integrity, diligence and discretion of...," followed by my name—the name of a homosexual, of a person who, according to his country's Immigration and Naturalization Service, does not even "possess the good moral character required for citizenship."

Homosexual relationships pose a special set of problems for the legal profession: On what basis does the law refuse to allow homosexuals to marry, file joint income tax returns, and adopt children? Although these problems admittedly concern only a small minority of the homosexual population—the crucial struggle is for the repeal of laws that discriminate against homosexuals in employment and housing—they are, nevertheless, an integral part of the fight for equality under the law.

Jack Baker and Michael McConnell are a homosexual couple whose desire to be legally married has resulted in a number of legal actions that illuminate the conflict between homosexuality and the law. Jack is a thirty-two-year-old graduate of the University of Minnesota Law School. An open homosexual, he was elected president of the University of Minnesota Student Association; he was admitted to the Minnesota bar in 1972. Michael, also thirty-two, is a librarian. He was fired from his job at the University of Minnesota library in 1971, not because he is a homosexual per se but because his marriage to Jack that year was construed as being an excessively militant act. (Jack took the university's Board of Regents to court in a suit for Michael's job, claiming that his dismissal from public employment because of his sexual preference was unconstitutional. He won the suit in the Federal District Court, but lost when the Board of Regents appealed the decision to the Eighth District Court of Appeals.)

Jack and Michael had been living together as lovers for nearly three years when, on New Year's Eve, 1969, they decided they wanted to get married. The idea made sense to them as lovers, as activists, and as practical people who looked ahead to such matters as inheritance rights and property privileges. They both felt that their love was as valid and deep as that uniting any heterosexual couple, and that both the state and society should recognize it as such. They also felt that they could win a new dignity and self-respect for other homosexuals if they set a precedent by legally marrying.

Jack and Michael applied for a marriage license in May 1970 at a Minnesota county clerk's office. When the county attorney denied their application, they took their case to court; the state's marriage laws, they argued, did not specify that persons applying for a marriage license must be of different genders. No, but that certainly was the overall intent of the laws, argued the two judges in lower courts who ruled against them; and their rulings were subsequently upheld by the Minnesota Supreme Court.

In the summer of 1971 Jack and Michael took a different route. Michael legally adopted Jack; Jack legally changed his name to Pat Lyn—a name that could be construed as that of either a man or a woman—and Michael then applied alone, as can be done in Minnesota, for a marriage license for himself and Pat Lyn McConnell. The unsuspecting clerk issued the license. On September 3, 1971, the two men were married by a Methodist minister who was a friend of theirs—and who was later reprimanded by his superior. There is nothing in the annals of the law prohibiting a person from marrying a person he or she has adopted. Michael and Jack's marriage is, in their own words, "America's first legally recognized same-sex marriage."

Since their marriage, Michael and Jack have annually

filed joint income tax returns. The Internal Revenue Service has yet to rule on whether it will accept their returns. Filing a joint return, meanwhile, has not proved financially advantageous, as the couple had hoped it would. Both men work—Michael has taken a job with a municipal library, Jack practices law—and although married couples pay a lower federal tax rate than singles do on the same income, the graduated nature of the income tax rate resulted in the couple's having to pay $162 more in 1973 than they would have paid as single men. Jack, alias Pat Lyn, says that he and Michael "have no choice but to file as married and pay the penalty, lest we be liable for perjury or ruin our marriage claim in court."

Jack and Michael have recently applied to adopt a child. If they are granted permission, they will be setting another precedent. Covertly homosexual men have, of course, reared children—their own or adopted children or foster children—and a few openly homosexual men have served as foster parents for runaway homosexual adolescents. So far, however, no openly homosexual man has been permitted to adopt a child. The two reasons that are usually produced give way under the least pressure—that homosexuals are too sick or unstable to rear children, and that homosexuals are child molesters.

While Jack and Michael await the outcome of their application to adopt, the courts have been dealing with another aspect of homosexuality and parental rights. A number of court decisions have held that the mere fact that a parent is homosexual is not sufficient reason to declare him or her unfit to have custody of the children of a broken marriage. Lesbian mothers have generally been granted custody of their children, but then the courts have always tended to grant custody of children to the mother. In 1973 the Court of Appeals of Oregon refused to remove two sons from the custody of their homosexual father,

235

finding that the boys' welfare was not being adversely affected by their living with him. (The American Civil Liberties Union believes that this is probably the only case in which a known homosexual father has fought in the courts for the custody of his children.) Most court cases involving homosexual fathers concern visitation rights. The two cases that have attracted the most attention are those of Jerry Purpura, president of the Gay Activists Alliance of New Jersey, in 1972, and Dr. Bruce Voeller, president of the Gay Activists Alliance of New York and executive director of the National Gay Task Force, in 1973. Both live with male lovers. The challenge to their visitation rights was not made because of their homosexuality per se, but because of the publicity surrounding it and the fact that they insisted on their lovers' joining them in the visits. In both cases the courts have severely limited the men's visitation rights. Moreover, Purpura must have a court-approved chaperon present when his children are with him, Voeller cannot keep his overnight, and the fathers' lovers have both been excluded from any visits.

Since Stonewall, the main goal of gay activists has been to persuade legislators to add homosexuals to the list of minorities protected by antidiscrimination laws. In most cases this can be accomplished by including the words "sexual preference" or "affectional preference" in those human rights statutes that now mention only race, creed, and sex.

There is a paradoxical element in the activists' fight. Although most homosexuals fear that they will be fired or ostracized if their sexual preference is revealed, it is the rare homosexual who is actually discriminated against on the job or when trying to rent an apartment or buy a house, and the reason for this is that most homosexuals conceal their sexual preference. But as more people come out publicly, the potential for discrimination against them increases. The vicious circle again: If they do come out—as they must in order to publicly advocate the passage of antidiscrimination laws and to show how many of them there are—they may well be fired. It is concealment and acceptance of second-class citizenship that seem to be rewarded, and openness and protest punished. Consequently, most homosexuals will probably not come out at least until the active minority has secured job protection for them.

In the meantime, the constant pushing and demonstrating and protesting and lobbying of this open and very vocal minority have been responsible for the passage of antidiscrimination laws in a number of cities—Ann Arbor, Berkeley, Columbus, Detroit, East Lansing, Minneapolis, Saint Paul, San Francisco, Seattle, and Washington, D.C., among others.

The most vehement and protracted public discussion over gay rights legislation has taken place in New York City, where legislation has been introduced each year since 1971. When a gay rights bill was at last voted out of committee, in 1974, it was defeated by the City Council by only three votes.

I have, of course, closely followed these proceedings, as I have similar legislative fights throughout the country. Almost invariably, the same three basic objections to the passage of these antidiscrimination laws are brought forward. And, as I have learned from speaking before straight audiences in various parts of the country, the thinking that lies behind these objections is widely shared by the general public. I shall take up these three points in the order of their importance.

1. *Homosexuals molest children and must therefore be excluded from jobs that involve contact with children.* All authoritative studies of this problem, including that

237

made by the Kinsey Institute,* conclude that child molesting is properly viewed as a category distinct from homosexuality and heterosexuality, although the overwhelming majority of offenders have a heterosexual background. These studies also show that the majority of those apprehended for molesting boys have also molested girls. Pedophiles, to give child molesters their technical name, are not homosexuals, do not regard themselves as homosexuals, and are not even on the fringes of the homosexual community. (One would think that educators would by now have educated themselves on this subject, but of course it is in the field of education that homosexuals are most likely to be discriminated against, on the grounds that they will inevitably molest their male pupils. In New York City there are many teachers who are secretly homosexual. Yet there have been far fewer cases reported of male teachers molesting boys than of male teachers molesting girls.)

2. *Giving homosexuals full civil rights would increase the number of homosexuals.* There is no scientific evidence whatsoever to support this statement. Obviously, assuring homosexuals of their full rights as citizens would allow many covert homosexuals to come out, thus increasing the number of those who could be counted, but it would certainly not influence the sexual orientation of children, which all authorities agree is fixed by the age of six or seven.

Indeed, it is difficult to understand the reasoning of those who raise this objection to granting homosexuals their full rights.

3. *Giving homosexuals full civil rights would encourage public transvestism.* This commonly voiced fear is based on the widely held notion that most transvestites are

* P. Gebhard, J. Gagnon, W. Pomeroy, and C. Christensen, *Sex Offenders* (New York: Harper & Row, 1965), p. 272.

homosexual. Although it is even more difficult to obtain accurate data about transvestites than about homosexuals, Dr. Kinsey found "only a few isolated cases of transvestism" among a group of nearly 2,000 homosexuals, and only a few isolated cases of homosexuality among the transvestite histories he compiled.* The leaders of New York City transvestite groups tell me that their memberships are predominantly heterosexual. Gay activists support transvestites, whom they see as yet another minority deprived of their full civil rights, as a matter of principle. But many homosexuals are as antitransvestite as are straight men and women. They do not enjoy being lumped together with men who reinforce the effeminate stereotype even though they are not homosexual.

Which of the three great oppressors—psychiatry, the church, and the law—has done the greatest harm to the homosexual's sense of himself? I don't know. It is difficult to isolate the three, so frequently are they used to reinforce one another. Psychiatric opinions are used as freely as the moral judgments that underlie them to back up oppressive laws.

In my own case, psychiatry was the worst villain, perhaps because my exposure to it was much greater than that of most homosexuals. For the majority of homosexuals, it is the law that has caused the most damage, for laws represent the judgment of society—the people we must live with. The defeat of antidiscrimination laws means to me, as it must to all homosexuals, that the community we live in still cannot regard us as fully human. The passage of such laws would mean that our community has finally come to understand that we, too, deserve to be granted the basic rights shared by all other citizens.

* Wardell P. Pomeroy, *Doctor Kinsey and the Institute for Sexual Research* (New York: Harper & Row, 1972), p. 323.

Until the early 1970's I had not heard a single intellectual or social leader speak out for tolerance, much less acceptance, of homosexuals. At the 1974 New York City Council hearings, however, a procession of leaders in the fields of law, public health, and labor, and a number of elected officials and leading intellectuals explained why they supported the passage of the gay rights bill—and for the first time in my life, I felt that I was truly included in our society. In my own testimony, I tried to explain what passage of the bill before the council would mean to me and to other homosexuals:

When the City Council passes this legislation—and I say when, for it will be passed, if not now, then someday—the only change you will notice will be the rejoicing of those who have come down here and lobbied. Firemen will not announce in their firehouses that they are homosexual; policemen riding in their cars will not turn to their buddies and say they're homosexual; teachers will not tell their classes they are homosexual; the New York *Times* will not be flooded with people announcing they are homosexual.

Most homosexuals will remain as they were, simply because most people don't talk publicly about their sex life anyway.

But with this legislation you will have affirmed that you believe homosexuals have the right to work, live, and just be—every day. And in so doing, you will have freed us from some of our anxieties.

The most important thing is that the hundreds of thousands of homosexuals in this city will feel the warmth of your decency, which is something they never expected to feel.

Do this for all of us. You have already done it for me personally by your acceptance of me since I came out openly as a homosexual. And you would do it for them if you knew them. But you do. They are your neighbors and your friends. Life is too short to make them wait any longer.

# CHAPTER THIRTEEN

# Epilogue: The Future

The gay civil rights movement is gradually redefining society's view of homosexuals; even more importantly, it is helping us to see ourselves in a new light. As conditions change, we, too, are changing.

From the reactions of many straight people to my coming out publicly and from my meetings with young gay leaders from Maine to Hawaii ever since, I have good reason to believe that our future will be very different from the damaging past. I realize that the typical reactions of straight New Yorkers are apt to be more sophisticated than those of people in parts of the country where minorities are less in evidence; I also realize that, as a doctor, professor, and former public official, I could expect, as less well known homosexuals could not, to be treated politely by the media. But the response to my announcement went far beyond politeness. I received an outpouring of support —from neighbors, friends, colleagues, and students.

As it turned out, straight people *did* understand my urge to come forward, to put behind me a life of fear. Many even understood the political implications of my speech—that I was trying to call the public's attention to the fact that many physicians and other professionals are gay and that we are all very much like everyone else. In no time I became aware of a fund of good will and sympathetic understanding that I had not known existed. Indeed, I discovered—it was a shock to me—that many straight people were more accepting of gays than I myself had been.

I had never stopped to consider how oppressed I was by my need to conceal my homosexuality. I saw now that I could be much more open with my straight colleagues and friends, that I could talk to them for the first time about my home life. Throughout those wasted years, whenever I had been walking with a straight person and saw a gay friend, I had tensed up to warn him by word or glance that my companion was straight and that he would have to be very careful. (In the 1950's the unwritten rule for such encounters was that the gay men would pass each other in silence, like total strangers.) Now we could stop and talk. In short, we could behave like human beings.

But there are legacies from the past that have stayed with me. I still cannot help seeing myself as inherently inferior to others; it is very hard to outgrow a belief that so many voices have reinforced for so many years. I was still very much the gay Uncle Tom when I made my public annoucement. Yes, we should all have our rights, but only so long as we behaved properly—behaved, that is, like respectable professionals, wore suits and ties, and never showed affection in public. Somehow I felt that we had to behave *more* properly than straights—be *more* moral. Since we did not really deserve our rights, I reasoned, we would have to work especially hard to earn them. George Orwell's sardonic *Animal Farm* slogan, "All men are equal, but some are more equal than others," rang in my ears. We were obviously less equal than heterosexual men.

If my generation of gay men is on the whole reluctant to come out publicly, it is largely because they continue to accept society's view of them. One must believe in one's own worth, after all, before one can fight for one's rights. It is not fear alone that keeps so many hidden and silent. Very few gay men my age are willing to contribute money to the gay cause, even anonymously. For many, the struggle to survive emotionally has been so debilitating that they have no energy left to reach out to others. By remaining in hiding they have allowed a portion of their humanity to be taken from them. From the point of view of their ability to serve, they are a lost generation. Gay psychiatrists sat silent as the APA debated whether the sickness label should be removed. Gay priests in New York City obediently read from the pulpit letters denouncing the gay civil rights bill that would have helped so many homosexuals. Gay politicians have refrained from taking a stand on gay rights legislation. Security comes first; service can wait.

The new gays—the young activists I met on college campuses and in large cities and a few small towns throughout America—are a different breed.

Shortly after I came out publicly, I set off on a speaking tour that took me around the country. Brainwashed into accepting many of society's stereotypes, I expected the young activists I would be meeting to be affected, effeminate, inept, irresponsible. How relieved I was when I met them! They were articulate and bright, and having accepted and come to terms with their homosexuality, they were able to be natural and open. They appeared to be as diverse as any other group of young men. Some were strong and athletic-looking, others slight; some were on their college football and baseball teams, others were editors of their college newspapers or played in the band. Like students everywhere, most of them wore jeans. Lovers were not self-conscious about holding hands, and straight students spoke with them as naturally as they did with other members of the college community. Aware that my own impressions of these young men might be suspect, I introduced several of them who came to New York for a Gay Pride Week march to my straight friends. Their reactions were much like mine. As one put it: "They look like campus leaders." Another remarked, "These guys aren't hiding, but they're not pushing their gayness on you, either. They're very natural, very likable, in fact."

It is this naturalness that most distinguishes them from the predominantly inward-looking, self-doubting, guilt-ridden, and frightened gay students of my generation. How did they get that way? Most of these young activists were just beginning to face their homosexuality when they came to college. There they found acceptance. Since the Stonewall riots of 1969, gay students have been forming groups on campus, where their work and their mere presence have effected a profound change. Some 200 of the nation's approximately 1,000 gay groups are student groups.

In my home state of Ohio, Kent State University recognizes the Kent Gay Liberation Front as an official student activity, provides it with office space, and allots it a small portion of the general student activity fund. As gay students are allowed to hold parties and dances on campus, their social life can now take place officially within the context of the college community. Some teachers have come out publicly, among them Dr. Dolores Noll, a forty-four-year-old professor of medieval literature who made her announcement in 1971. Today she serves as faculty adviser for the Kent Gay Liberation Front, whose membership has grown in the past three years from less than a dozen to more than fifty. She also teaches a credit course titled "Politics of Gay Liberation." Another homosexual instructor, William Hoover, teaches a credit course titled "Sociology of Devi-

244

ance." At Kent—as at most colleges and universities and within many gay activist groups—lesbians and homosexual men are friends and allies, and sometimes even roommates. This sort of friendship was totally unknown to my generation.

Another Ohio college, Oberlin, has accepted its gay students to the extent of having an open homosexual on the staff of the student counseling center. In 1974, several members of the psychology department participated in a weekend-long seminar on homosexuality, at which I was the keynote speaker. The chairman of the department, Professor John Thompson, gave a speech on the normality —in all but a statistical sense—of homosexual and bisexual behavior, and other department members spoke on various aspects of human sexual behavior. Several department members and their wives turned up at the Saturday night dance given by the gay students, as did many heterosexual student couples. In fact, about half of those present were straight—an indication of the ease with which straights and open gays get along on many campuses today.

The new gays, of course, are found not only on college campuses, though it was there that I first became aware of them. They are also found in the nation's 800 or so off-campus gay activist groups and counseling centers. Like their college counterparts, most of these young activists accepted their gayness without having to undergo the protracted struggle men of my generation went through, and without having to spend the seemingly endless hours that we spent to find a gay community. They have the emotional security—and the energy—to serve others.

These new gays are providing services that will aid individual homosexuals and bring about change for all homosexuals. In a number of cities, gay lawyers have established low-cost legal clinics. In New York City, young gay nurses and physicians have set up free clinics for gays who cannot afford to go to private physicians. The Gay Nurses Association, which was founded in 1973 in Philadelphia by two young nurses and now has chapters in more than twenty cities, helps gay nurses, male as well as female, to accept themselves, and educates straight nurses about homosexuality. Meanwhile, other activists concentrate on lobbying for changes in the laws.

I am aware that gays drawing together in groups are in a sense seceding from straight society. By emphasizing the need for young gays to join such groups I am, I can see, advocating gay separatism—for a time, at least. Just as blacks have had to form exclusively black organizations to find out who they are and what their goals are, so must we. We need to join together in gay clubs, gay churches, and gay service agencies, to help undo the damage done to our sense of ourselves through years of hostility and rejection by society. Seeing many gay people in positions of service will help eradicate the image some of us have of ourselves as self-centered and shallow—an image that to some extent may have represented past generations of men who, preoccupied with their guilts and fears, withdrew into themselves or restricted their interests to those of a closed circle.

I believe it will take the rest of this century for society to rid itself of its prejudice against homosexuals. A new generation of homosexual men and women will have to grow up secure in their identity, knowing from the start that gay people can be happy, loving, and of value to society. And a new generation of straight men and women will have to grow up never having doubted that gay people are people.